EVERYDAY
NOT-SO-CRAP
FAMILY
MEALS

THE AUSTRALIAN
Women's Weekly

JESSICA ROWE

SMEG

Contents

Confessions of a Crap Housewife

Never in my wildest Crap-Housewife dreams did I imagine having a cookbook! Especially one with the iconic Australian Women's Weekly, who have been creating meals for Aussie families forever. (I remember my Mum had their classic 1970's cookbook.)

I've never been a domestic goddess – the smoke alarm goes off when I cook! I'm a huge fan of sauces that come in jars and microwave rice. I'd rather spend time making hats to match my meals instead of cooking. That's why this cookbook has everyday meals full of heart with lots of shortcuts. And there's plenty of sweetness here too, because life is too short not to enjoy dessert.

Remember it's okay to have cereal for dinner sometimes! And never forget you are enough.

xx Jess

Sugar

Dinners My Family Will ~~Actually~~ Mostly Eat

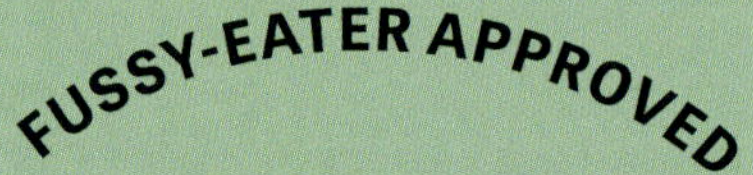

Sticky (*not burnt*) chicken with noodles

PREP + COOK TIME 15 MINUTES

CHICKEN HAS A HABIT OF TURNING TO CHARCOAL IN MY KITCHEN! BUT IT WON'T IF YOU FOLLOW THESE SIMPLE STEPS FOR A FOOLPROOF TASTY MEAL.

SERVES 4

2 green onions
1 long red chilli
400g leafy Asian greens
1 medium red capsicum
600g chicken thigh fillets
½ tsp Chinese five-spice powder
2 tsp brown sugar
2 tbsp sweet chilli sauce
1 tbsp kecap manis
1 tbsp soy sauce
1 tbsp olive oil
200g baby corn
440g shelf-fresh hokkien noodles
2 tbsp roasted peanuts
coriander leaves, to serve

Thinly slice green onion and chilli. Cut Asian greens into long lengths. Remove seeds from capsicum and cut into slices. Thickly slice chicken.

Combine chicken, spice, sugar and half of each of the sauces in a bowl.

Heat a large wok (or frying pan) over high heat, add the oil; stir-fry chicken mixture, baby corn and capsicum, in batches, for 3 mins or until vegies are charred and chicken is browned, cooked through and sticky. (According to cooking friends, the trick here is to not overcrowd the wok.) Transfer to a bowl. Wipe wok clean.

Add greens and 2 tbsp water to the wok; stir-fry for 1 min or until greens are just tender. Add remaining sauces; stir-fry for 1 min or until heated through. Add noodles to wok; toss gently until just combined.

Serve noodle mixture topped with chicken mixture, green onion, chilli, peanuts and coriander.

ROCKSTAR INGREDIENT Shelf-fresh noodles are ready to hit the wok and don't need to be cooked. Even I can't mess this up!

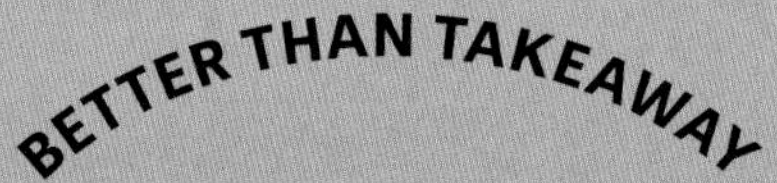

Magic mince beef empanadas

PREP + COOK TIME 1 HOUR 20 MINUTES (+ COOLING)

MINCE IS A HIGHLY UNDER-RATED STYLE OF MEAT. IT'S ALMOST IMPOSSIBLE TO BURN OR OVERCOOK AND YOU CAN KEEP REINVENTING THE WAYS YOU USE THIS MAGICAL INGREDIENT.

SERVES 4

2 tbsp extra virgin olive oil
1 onion, chopped finely
3 cloves garlic, chopped finely
100g cured chorizo sausage, diced finely
1 red capsicum, chopped finely
500g beef mince
2 tsp ground cumin
2 tsp smoked paprika
¼ cup (40g) currants
400g can diced tomatoes
1 tbsp tomato paste
8 sheets frozen shortcrust pastry, thawed
1 egg, beaten lightly
coriander leaves, to serve

Preheat oven to 200°C/180°C fan-forced. Line a large oven tray with baking paper.

Heat oil in a large non-stick frying pan over high heat. Add the onion; cook for 3 mins or until softened. Add garlic, chorizo and capsicum; cook, stirring, for 4 mins or until capsicum is softened.

Add beef to pan; cook, stirring with a wooden spoon to break up any lumps, for 8 mins or until browned. Stir in the spices; cook for 1 min or until fragrant. Add currants, canned tomatoes, tomato paste and ½ cup (125ml) water. Bring to the boil; cook for 10 mins or until mixture thickens. Leave to cool to room temperature.

Using a plate as a guide, cut an 18cm round from a pastry sheet. Top with an eighth of beef filling in centre. Brush a little egg around edge of pastry. Fold pastry round in half to enclose filling, place on prepared tray and use a fork to press edges together to seal; brush top with egg. Repeat with remaining pastry, filling and egg to make 8 empanadas.

Bake empanadas for 30 mins or until golden underneath. Serve with coriander leaves.

MID-WEEK WINNER

Going-to-plan stroganoff

PREP + COOK TIME 30 MINUTES

MUM USED TO MAKE 'STROG' WHEN WE WERE GROWING UP. HERE IS A SLIGHTLY FANCIER VERSION AS NO PACKET IS INVOLVED IN THE MAKING OF THIS SAUCE!

SERVES 4-6

500g rigatoni pasta
2 tbsp olive oil
600g beef sirloin, sliced thinly
20g butter
1 onion, sliced thinly
2 cloves garlic, crushed
375g button mushrooms, halved if large
2 tbsp plain flour
⅓ cup (80ml) brandy
2 cups (500ml) beef stock
1 cup (240g) sour cream
¼ cup chopped flat-leaf parsley
smoked paprika, to serve

Cook the pasta in a large saucepan of salted boiling water following packet directions until tender; drain.

Meanwhile, heat the oil in a large frying pan over high heat; cook beef, in batches, for 30 secs on each side or until browned. Remove the beef from pan; cover to keep warm.

Melt the butter in same pan; cook onion, garlic and mushrooms, stirring occasionally, for 5 mins or until softened. Add the flour; cook, stirring, for 1 min. Add brandy; cook, stirring, for 30 secs. Add stock; bring to the boil. Reduce heat to low; cook for 5 mins. Return beef to pan with sour cream; stir until smooth. Remove from heat; season. Add three-quarters of the parsley; stir until combined.

Serve pasta topped with stroganoff and the remaining parsley. Sprinkle with paprika.

CAN'T BE BOTHERED Ask your butcher to slice the beef for you or buy beef stir-fry strips. Swap garlic cloves for 1½ tsp garlic paste.

BARELY ANY PREP

On-special minestrone with ravioli

PREP + COOK TIME 25 MINUTES

KEEP THIS SUPER SIMPLE BY USING PRE-CUT VEGIES FROM THE SUPERMARKET, WHAT'S ON SPECIAL OR ANY LEFTOVERS IN THE FRIDGE. GOOD FOR YOU AND THE ENVIRONMENT!

SERVES 4

2 tbsp extra virgin olive oil
1 large onion, chopped finely
2 cloves garlic, crushed
1 tbsp finely chopped rosemary leaves
1 large carrot, chopped finely
2 trimmed celery stalks, chopped finely
2 x 400g cans diced tomatoes
1 litre (4 cups) vegetable stock
1 tsp caster sugar
400g fresh mini beef ravioli
shaved parmesan and curly parsley, to serve

Heat oil in a medium saucepan over medium heat. Cook onion, garlic, rosemary, carrot and celery, stirring, for 5 mins or until softened.

Add tomatoes, stock and sugar to pan; season. Bring to the boil; cook for 5 mins. Add ravioli; cook for 5 mins or until ravioli is tender.

Divide minestrone among bowls. Top with the parmesan and parsley; season with pepper.

TIPS Ravioli is available from the refrigerated section of most supermarkets. For a vegetarian option, use spinach and ricotta ravioli. If you plan to freeze the soup, don't add the ravioli.

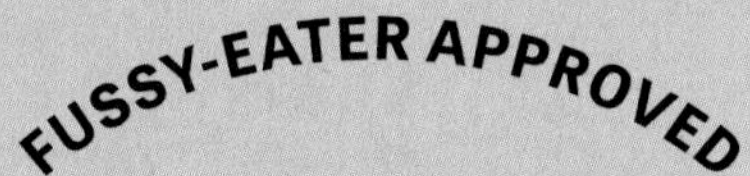

Frying-pan beef lasagne *I love you*

PREP + COOK TIME 20 MINUTES

PASTA AND READY-MADE INGREDIENTS. AND IT'S COOKED IN ONE PAN! THIS IS A MIRACLE IN A PAN WHICH MY WHOLE FAMILY ENJOYS EATING. PLUS THERE'S MINIMAL WASHING UP.

SERVES 6

- **1 tbsp extra virgin olive oil**
- **1 large onion, chopped finely**
- **2 cloves garlic, crushed**
- **375g packet fresh lasagne sheets**
- **60g baby spinach leaves**
- **900g ready-made fresh Bolognese pasta sauce with beef**
- **1½ cups (360g) firm ricotta, crumbled**
- **1½ cups (150g) grated pizza cheese**
- **basil leaves, to serve (optional)**

Heat oil in a large, deep frying pan with a tight-fitting lid over medium-high heat; cook onion and garlic, stirring, for 5 mins or until onion softens.

Meanwhile, tear lasagne sheets lengthways into strips; put long strips aside, save any small broken pieces. Sprinkle small broken pasta pieces and the spinach into pan with onion; mix gently to combine. Pour combined pasta sauce and 1½ cups (375ml) water into pan; mix to combine.

Place long pasta strips, standing upright on long sides as pictured, into the mixture. Bring to the boil over high heat. Cover pan with lid, reduce heat to low; cook, covered, for 5 mins or until pasta is tender.

Meanwhile, preheat grill. Uncover pan, sprinkle with both cheeses. Grill for 5 mins or until cheese melts.

Season lasagne with pepper. Top with basil, if using.

CAN'T BE BOTHERED There's no shame in using ready-made refrigerated Bolognese pasta sauce with beef and herbs; it's available from the refrigerated section of most supermarkets.

MID-WEEK WINNER

Chicken pie doesn't lie

PREP + COOK TIME 45 MINUTES (+ COOLING)

THE JOY OF THE BBQ CHOOK. PLUS IF THE LEEK BUSINESS IS TOO FUSSY, LEAVE IT OUT AND JUST MIX THE SOUP MIXTURE AND CREAM WITH THE CHOOK. I OFTEN DO!

SERVES 6

1 barbecue chicken (900g)
60g butter, chopped
1 large leek, sliced thinly
2 stalks celery, trimmed, chopped finely
2 tbsp plain flour
2 tsp thyme leaves, plus extra to serve
420g can condensed cream of chicken soup
1 cup (250ml) pouring cream
1 tbsp wholegrain mustard
1 sheet frozen puff pastry, thawed
1 egg yolk, beaten lightly

Preheat oven to 200°C/180°C fan-forced. Grease a deep, 23cm, 1.5-litre (6-cup) square ovenproof dish.

Remove skin from chicken then pull off the meat in large chunks. Coarsely chop chicken (or break with your hands); you will have about 3 cups (480g).

Heat butter in a medium saucepan; cook leek and celery, stirring, for 5 mins or until softened. Add flour and thyme; cook, stirring, for 1 min. Gradually stir in the soup and cream; cook, stirring, for 3 mins or until mixture boils and thickens. Stir in chopped chicken and the mustard. Season to taste. Cool for 15 mins.

Spoon chicken mixture into dish; place puff pastry over filling, trim to fit dish. Brush pastry with the egg yolk.

Bake pie for 20 mins or until pastry is puffed and browned. Serve sprinkled with salt and extra thyme.

LEFTOVERS Take two slices of bread and pile high with pie filling; place in a sandwich press or jaffle maker and toast for 4 mins.

MICROWAVE KICKSTART

Pumpkin & corn quiche boats

PREP + COOK TIME 45 MINUTES

OMG THESE TASTY MORSELS ARE A REVELATION. A BIT FANCY PANTS AND OPEN FOR REINTERPRETATION WITH DIFFERENT FILLINGS.

MAKES 12

- **12 mini soft Stand 'n Stuff tortillas**
- **300g store-bought diced butternut pumpkin**
- **2 slices ham of choice**
- **1 green onion, plus extra to serve**
- **125g can corn kernels**
- **2 tbsp taco seasoning**
- **1 cup (120g) grated Mexican cheese blend**
- **3 eggs**
- **½ cup (125ml) pouring cream**
- **guacamole and sour cream, to serve**

Preheat oven to 200°C/180°C fan-forced. Line a large oven tray with baking paper. Place tortillas on tray.

Check the pumpkin pieces for size – they should all be approx. 1cm cubes. Place in a microwave-safe bowl and cover with wet paper towel. Microwave on HIGH for 5 mins, gently stirring pumpkin halfway through cooking, or until just tender. Transfer the pumpkin to a large bowl.

Finely chop the ham and thinly slice green onion. Drain the corn. Add ham, green onion and corn to pumpkin with taco seasoning and cheese. Gently fold to combine, being careful not to break up pumpkin.

Crack eggs into a large jug. Add cream, then season. Using a fork, beat until combined.

Divide pumpkin mixture evenly among tortillas. Carefully pour over the egg mixture.

Bake the quiches for 20 mins or until egg mixture is set and lightly browned.

Serve quiches topped with guacamole, sour cream and extra green onion. Season with pepper.

ROCKSTAR INGREDIENT Stand 'n Stuff tortillas are a saviour – the crisp shells mean you can say 'goodbye' to soggy pastry bottoms.

Taco Tuesday – beefy style

PREP + COOK TIME 30 MINUTES

EVERY DAY IS TACO DAY FOR US! I MEAN WHO DOESN'T LOVE A TACO? YOU CAN PICK AND CHOOSE WHAT INGREDIENTS TO ADD SO IT'S PERFECT FOR THE FUSSIEST EATERS. AND I HAVE A MATCHING TACO HAT FOR THE OCCASION.

SERVES 4

1 tbsp extra virgin olive oil
1 clove garlic, crushed
500g beef mince
2 tbsp tomato paste
2 tsp sweet paprika
1 tsp ground cumin
12 corn taco shells
2 medium tomatoes
8 cos lettuce leaves
200g store-bought guacamole
1 cup (120g) coarsely grated cheddar

Preheat oven to 180°C/160°C fan-forced.

Heat oil in a large frying pan over medium heat. Add garlic and beef. Cook, stirring with a wooden spoon to break up any lumps, for 5 mins or until beef is browned. Add tomato paste, paprika and cumin to pan; stir for 1 min. Stir in 1½ cups (375ml) water; season with salt and pepper. Bring to the boil, then reduce heat. Simmer for 10 mins or until most of the liquid evaporates.

Meanwhile, place taco shells on a large oven tray. Place tray in the oven for 5 mins or until taco shells are warmed.

Finely chop tomato and finely shred lettuce.

Divide mince mixture among taco shells, then top with guacamole, tomato, lettuce and cheddar.

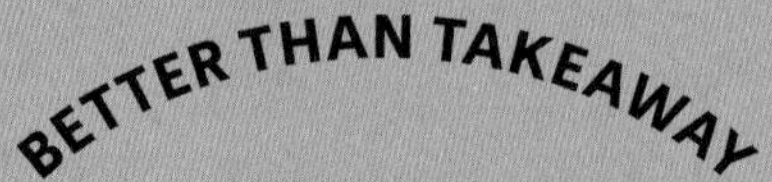

Mermaid meal with pearls (*fish & chips*)

PREP + COOK TIME 40 MINUTES

MERMAIDS HAVE A SPECIAL PLACE IN MY HEART. DID YOU KNOW I DRESSED UP LIKE A MERMAID FOR MY FIRST DATE WITH MY NOW HUSBAND!

SERVES 4

2 large orange sweet potatoes, unpeeled, cut into thin wedges
1 tbsp vegetable oil
1 tbsp ground cumin
1 tbsp ground coriander
1 tsp ground turmeric
2 tsp salt flakes
¼ cup (40g) sesame seeds
⅔ cup (50g) panko (Japanese) breadcrumbs
½ cup (150g) mayonnaise
800g skinless, boneless firm white fish fillets (see tip)
olive oil cooking spray
steamed peas, lemon wedges and tartare sauce, to serve

Preheat oven to 200°C/180°C fan-forced. Line two oven trays with baking paper.

Place sweet potato on one lined tray; drizzle with oil then spread out in a single layer. Season. Bake for 20 mins or until browned lightly, cooked through and crisp on the outside.

Meanwhile, combine the spices, salt, sesame seeds and breadcrumbs in a wide shallow bowl. Place the mayonnaise in another shallow bowl. Coat fish fillets in mayonnaise, wipe off any excess. Place fish in the breadcrumb mixture, turning to coat. Place on second lined tray; repeat with remaining fish. Spray crumbed fish generously with cooking oil spray.

Bake fish for 12 mins or until golden and cooked through. Serve fish with sweet potato wedges, peas, lemon wedges and tartare sauce.

TIP Fish to try are: flathead fillets, snapper, ling, whiting or blue-eye trevalla.

AIR FRYER FANTASTIC

Crumb vegies & they will eat them!

PREP + COOK TIME 40 MINUTES

OH IT'S BORING NAGGING KIDS AND GROWN UPS TO EAT VEGIES. I'VE DISCOVERED THAT ANYTHING CRUMBED AND PUT IN THE AIR FRYER WILL BE EATEN.

SERVES 4

You will need an air fryer for this recipe.

⅓ cup (50g) linseed (flaxseed) meal
½ cup (140g) Dijon mustard
1⅔ cups (250g) plain flour
2 tsp onion powder
2 tsp garlic powder
2 tsp smoked paprika
½ tsp hot stuff (cayenne pepper or chilli powder)
½ medium cauliflower, cut into 2.5cm florets
1 head broccoli, cut into 2.5cm florets
olive oil cooking spray
sauce of choice, to serve (mayonnaise, ketchup, hot sauce or warm pasta sauce)

Combine linseed meal with 1⅓ cups (330ml) water in a large bowl; stand for 5 mins or until thickened. Add mustard; stir to combine. Combine flour, onion powder, garlic powder and spices in another large bowl; season with salt.

Preheat a 5.3-litre air fryer to 180°C for 3 mins.

Add cauliflower and broccoli to linseed mixture; stir to coat. Working in batches, toss cauliflower and broccoli in flour mixture to coat; spray generously with oil.

Taking care, place half the vegies in the air-fryer basket; cook at 180°C for 10 mins, turning halfway through cooking, or until golden. Transfer to a bowl; season with salt and cover to keep warm. Repeat cooking with remaining vegies.

Serve crumbed vegies with sauce of choice.

HIDDEN VEGIES

Magic mince one-tray meatballs with spaghetti

PREP + COOK TIME 50 MINUTES

MINCE WORKS ITS MAGIC AGAIN! TRY CHICKEN MINCE THIS TIME AROUND OR YOU CAN ALWAYS GET THE MEATBALLS READY-MADE BY THE BUTCHER.

SERVES 4

1 cup (80g) frozen peas
2 tsp finely grated lemon rind
⅓ cup coarsely chopped parsley
500g chicken mince
2 cloves garlic, crushed
¼ cup (25g) dried breadcrumbs
1 egg
⅓ cup (80g) fresh ricotta
1 tbsp olive oil
2 x 400g cans diced tomatoes
3 tsp balsamic vinegar
500g spaghetti
2 tbsp finely grated parmesan
basil leaves and sliced baguette, to serve

Preheat oven to 240°C/220°C fan-forced. Line a shallow roasting pan with baking paper.

Place peas in a heatproof bowl; pour over enough boiling water from the kettle to cover. Stand peas for 1 min; drain. Blend or process peas, lemon rind and parsley until just combined. Add the chicken, garlic, breadcrumbs, egg and ricotta; pulse until combined.

Using wet hands (this will prevent the mixture sticking), roll level tablespoons of mixture into balls. Place in roasting pan; drizzle with oil. Roast meatballs for 15 mins, turning once. Add tomatoes and vinegar; roast for a further 15 mins or until the meatballs are cooked through and sauce is hot.

Meanwhile, cook pasta in a large saucepan of salted boiling water following packet directions until just tender. Drain.

Divide the pasta, meatballs and sauce among bowls. Top with parmesan and basil. Serve with bread.

PREP IT You can freeze the raw or cooked meatballs; thaw in the fridge before cooking or reheating.

BARELY ANY PREP

Fast beef Burgundy with pasta

PREP + COOK TIME 35 MINUTES

TASTY CUTS LIKE RUMP STEAK WON'T BREAK THE BUDGET. WHY NOT ASK YOUR BUTCHER TO DICE THE RUMP INTO EASY-TO-COOK SIZED PIECES.

SERVES 4

2 tbsp extra virgin olive oil
600g rump steak, trimmed, cut into 3cm pieces
100g streaky bacon, chopped
300g Swiss brown mushrooms, halved
2 cloves garlic, sliced thinly
2 tsp thyme leaves, plus extra to serve
2 tbsp tomato paste
1 tbsp plain flour
½ cup (125ml) red wine
1 cup (250ml) beef stock
300g short pasta of your choice

Heat 2 tsp of the olive oil in a large, deep, heavy-based frying pan over medium-high heat. Add half the beef; cook, stirring occasionally, for 4 mins or until browned on all sides. Transfer beef to a plate. Repeat with another 2 tsp of oil and remaining beef; transfer to plate.

Heat remaining oil in same pan; cook bacon and mushrooms over medium heat, stirring, for 3 mins. Add garlic; cook for 1 min. Add thyme and tomato paste; cook for 1 min. Add flour; cook, stirring, for a further 2 mins.

Add wine, bring to the boil over high heat; cook, stirring and scraping base of pan, for 2 mins or until wine is reduced by half (this is a good time for the cook to sample the quality of the wine). Add stock, bring to the boil; boil for 2 mins. Reduce heat to low, return beef to pan; simmer for 4 mins or until sauce is thickened and beef is tender.

Meanwhile, cook pasta in a large saucepan of salted boiling water following packet directions until just tender; drain.

Divide pasta and beef mixture among bowls; serve topped with extra thyme leaves.

AIR FRYER FANTASTIC

Everyone *loves* schnitzels & slaw

PREP + COOK TIME 40 MINUTES (+ REFRIGERATION)

THIS MEAL IS ON CONSTANT ROTATION IN OUR HOUSE. GIVE THE CHICKEN A GOOD WHACK BETWEEN BAKING PAPER TO FLATTEN BEFORE CRUMBING. I LOVE USING PANKO BREADCRUMBS AS THEY MAKE THE SCHNITZELS EXTRA GOLDEN AND CRISP. MY BESTIE DENISE DRYSDALE INTRODUCED ME TO THEM, SO I ALWAYS THINK OF HER WHEN I'M CRUMBING.

SERVES 4

You will need an air fryer for this recipe.

½ cup (75g) plain flour
2 eggs
⅓ cup (80ml) milk
2 cloves garlic, crushed
2 cups (150g) fresh breadcrumbs
⅓ cup (25g) finely grated parmesan
¼ cup chopped chives
1 tbsp finely chopped lemon thyme, plus extra to serve
2 tsp finely grated lemon rind (see tips)
500g chicken breasts, halved horizontally
olive oil cooking spray
520g coleslaw kit (see tips)

Place flour in a shallow bowl. Lightly beat eggs, milk and garlic in a second shallow bowl. Combine breadcrumbs, parmesan, chives, thyme and lemon rind in a third shallow bowl. Dust the chicken in flour, shaking off excess; dip in egg mixture, then coat in breadcrumb mixture. Place schnitzels on a plate. Refrigerate for 30 mins.

Preheat a 7-litre air fryer to 180°C for 3 mins.

Spray schnitzels generously on both sides with oil. Taking care, place half the schnitzels in the air-fryer basket; at 180°C, cook for 10 mins, turning halfway through the cooking time, or until golden and cooked through. Transfer to a plate; cover loosely with foil to keep warm. Repeat cooking with remaining schnitzels.

Season schnitzels with salt; sprinkle with extra thyme. Toss coleslaw with packet dressing and serve with schnitzels.

TIPS Cut the lemon that you've zested into wedges to serve. We used a coleslaw kit that included a dressing sachet.

ONE-POT WONDER

Chicken in a pot *(it must be good)*

PREP + COOK TIME 35 MINUTES

MY NERVES OFTEN GET THE BETTER OF ME WHEN I COOK CHICKEN. IS IT COOKED ENOUGH? TOO PINK? THIS RECIPE SHOULD KEEP YOU OUT OF THE DANGER ZONE.

SERVES 4

1 tbsp extra virgin olive oil
10 baby (chat) potatoes, halved
2 small red onions, quartered
4 cloves garlic, sliced
8 sprigs thyme
8 chicken thigh cutlets (1.2kg)
2 tbsp lemon juice
½ cup (125ml) dry white wine (try a cleanskin)
1 cup (250ml) chicken stock
250g truss cherry tomatoes, cut into clusters
100g baby spinach leaves
finely chopped flat-leaf parsley, to serve (optional)

Heat oil in a large casserole dish over medium heat. Add the potato and onion, cut-sides down; cook for 1½ mins each side or until browned. Add garlic and thyme; cook, stirring, until fragrant. Remove vegies and thyme from pan.

Make 3 deep cuts into the skin side of each cutlet. (Why? I have it on good authority this trick speeds up cooking and allows the flavour to permeate the chicken.) Heat same pan over high heat; cook chicken, skin-side down, for 2 mins. Turn, cook a further 2 mins or until browned. Top with vegie mixture.

Add lemon juice, wine and stock to pan; season well. Bring to the boil, reduce heat to medium; simmer, covered, for 10 mins. Add tomatoes; cook a further 5 mins or until chicken is cooked through and potato is tender. (Not sure if the chicken is cooked? Prod it with the tip of knife, the juices should run clear with no sign of blood.)

Remove from heat; stir in spinach. Serve casserole sprinkled with parsley, if using.

BARELY ANY PREP

On a wing & a prayer – *Hawaiian-style*

PREP + COOK TIME 1 HOUR (+ COOLING & OPTIONAL REFRIGERATION)

CHICKEN WINGS OFTEN GET BURNT IN MY OVEN. NOT SO WITH THIS SWEET RECIPE THAT'S FULL OF FLAVOUR AND WILL HAVE YOU SAYING ALOHA TO A MAI TAI.

SERVES 4

425g can pineapple rings in natural juices
3kg chicken wings
2 tbsp sweet paprika
425g corn cobbettes
curly parsley, to serve

MARINADE

⅔ cup (150g) firmly packed brown sugar
1 cup (250ml) fresh pineapple juice (see tip)
1 cup (280g) tomato sauce
1 cup (250ml) soy sauce
⅔ cup (160ml) malt vinegar
2 tbsp finely grated ginger or ginger paste
4 cloves garlic, crushed

To make the marinade, combine ingredients in a frying pan. Drain pineapple, add the juice to pan; reserve the pineapple. Bring marinade mixture to a simmer over medium heat; cook for 5 mins. Set aside to cool.

Place wings in a large bowl, sprinkling with paprika as you add them to the bowl. Pour over the marinade and toss well to coat. If time allows, refrigerate for 1-2 hours, tossing occasionally.

Preheat oven to 200°C/180°C fan-forced. Line two large oven trays with baking paper.

Divide pineapple between trays then lay chicken wings out over pineapple, leaving a little space at the end of each tray for the corn later. Roast for 45 mins, swapping trays between shelves halfway through cooking and adding corn to the tray for the last 15 mins of cooking time, or until both chicken and corn are cooked through.

Season with pepper, sprinkle with parsley and drizzle corn with any cooking juices to serve.

TIP Fresh pineapple juice is available from the chilled section of supermarkets.

MID-WEEK WINNER

Brekkie-for-dinner pasta

PREP + COOK TIME 30 MINUTES

SOMETIMES THERE'S NOTHING WRONG WITH CEREAL FOR DINNER. AND THIS MEAL TAKES THE IDEA UP A NOTCH. DON'T BE TOO PRECIOUS ABOUT USING ALL OF THESE INGREDIENTS. I'VE LEARNT TO PICK MY BATTLES WITH MY GIRLS AND EATING/NOT EATING EGGS ISN'T WORTH AN ARGUMENT.

SERVES 4

400g short or small pasta
2½ tbsp olive oil
3 fresh chorizo sausages (270g), casings removed, sliced
1 large red onion, cut into thin wedges
150g green vegies (see tip)
4 eggs
4 slices prosciutto (60g)
250g truss cherry tomatoes, cut into clusters
1 cup (240g) fresh ricotta
⅔ cup (50g) finely grated parmesan

Cook pasta in a large saucepan of salted boiling water, following packet directions until just tender. Drain, reserving ⅓ cup (80ml) cooking water.

Meanwhile, heat 2 tbsp of the oil in a large heavy-based frying pan over medium heat. Add chorizo and onion; cook, stirring, for 5 mins or until golden. Add green vegies; cook for 4 mins or until softened. Add reserved pasta water; season to taste.

Heat remaining 2 tsp oil in a large non-stick frying pan over medium heat. One at a time, crack eggs into pan; cook for 3 mins or until whites are set and yolks remain runny.

Preheat grill to high. Line an oven tray with baking paper. Place prosciutto and tomatoes on the tray; grill for 2 mins or until prosciutto is crisp and tomatoes soften.

Combine pasta, chorizo mixture and crumbled ricotta; divide among plates. Serve topped with prosciutto, eggs, tomatoes and parmesan; season with pepper.

TIP Try broccolini, cavolo nero, kale and spinach.

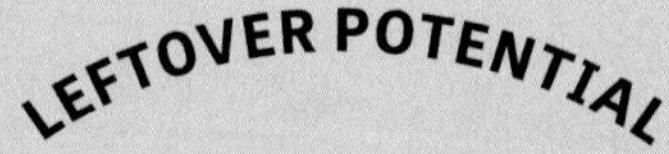

Easy lamb leg with a Moroccan-ish touch

PREP + COOK TIME 1½ HOURS

PERFECT FOR A WEEKEND LUNCH AND A CHANCE TO SIT AROUND THE TABLE TOGETHER. TRUTHFULLY, SINCE LIFE ISN'T A FAIRYTALE, THIS DOESN'T HAPPEN EVERY DAY IN OUR HOUSE.

SERVES 6

2kg bone-in leg of lamb
2 cloves garlic, crushed
2 tsp ground coriander
2 tsp ground cumin
1 tsp sweet paprika
¼ tsp ground turmeric
1kg waxy potatoes (eg Dutch cream), halved or quartered if large
3 small onions, peeled, quartered
1 cup (250ml) chicken stock
1 cup (280g) Greek yoghurt
1 Lebanese cucumber, chopped finely
handful of oregano and mint leaves, to serve (optional)

Preheat oven to 200°C/180°C fan-forced.

Place lamb in a large roasting pan. Rub surface with garlic, then rub with combined spices; season. Place potatoes and onions around the lamb in a single layer. Add stock to pan and season well.

Roast lamb and vegies for 15 mins; spoon pan juices over vegies. Reduce oven to 180°C/160°C fan-forced; roast a further 45 mins for medium. Insert a skewer or meat thermometer into the centre of the thickest part of the meat, away from the bone. It is cooked to medium when internal temperature reaches 65-70°C or when pink juices run from the meat.

Transfer lamb to a platter. Cover with foil; rest 15 mins. Turn vegies in pan juices; return to the oven. Roast a further 10 mins or until browned.

Add vegies to the platter with lamb. Serve with combined yoghurt and cucumber. If you're feeling fancy (and usually I'm not), scatter some oregano leaves over the meat and some mint over yoghurt.

TIP Check the pan during roasting to ensure the liquid hasn't evaporated; top up if necessary with a little extra stock or water.

Chicken satay skewers

PREP + COOK TIME 25 MINUTES (+ REFRIGERATION)

ANYTHING WITH PEANUT BUTTER AND COCONUT MILK IS A COMBO IN CULINARY HEAVEN. AND I ALWAYS USE THE MICROWAVE RICE IN A BAG. EASY AND MESS FREE!

SERVES 4

½ cup (140g) crunchy dark-roast peanut butter
165ml can coconut milk
2 tbsp soy sauce
1 tbsp brown sugar
1 tbsp lime juice
12 chicken tenderloins (900g)
12 bamboo skewers
steamed rice, chopped cucumber, lime wedges and coriander leaves, to serve

To make the marinade, place peanut butter, coconut milk, soy sauce, sugar and lime juice in a bowl. Stir until combined. If the marinade is too thick, add a splash of water.

Add chicken to marinade. Using tongs, turn the chicken to coat all over. Cover bowl and refrigerate for 1 hour.

Line a large oven tray with baking paper. Carefully thread each chicken piece onto a skewer. Place the skewers in neat rows on tray. Reserve remaining marinade in bowl.

Preheat grill to high.

Place tray under grill; cook chicken for 4 mins. Remove tray from grill; use tongs to turn skewers, return tray under grill. Cook a further 4 mins or until golden and cooked through.

Meanwhile, to make satay sauce, place reserved marinade in a small saucepan. Cook over medium heat, stirring, for 2 mins or until hot.

Serve chicken skewers with satay sauce, steamed rice, chopped cucumber, lime wedges and coriander.

CAN'T BE BOTHERED Don't worry about soaking the skewers. It's only worth doing if you're barbecuing.

HIDDEN VEGIES

Monday's mac 'n' cheese TV dinner

PREP + COOK TIME 45 MINUTES

CHECK OUT THIS INGENIOUS WAY OF HIDING CAULIFLOWER! HOW COULD ANYONE SAY NO TO THIS CHEESY, GOLDEN TREAT? PLUS PANKO BREADCRUMBS PLAY A STARRING ROLE.

SERVES 4

500g cauliflower, trimmed, cut into large florets
1 tbsp extra virgin olive oil
250g macaroni pasta
1 cup (240g) sour cream
1¼ cups (310ml) buttermilk
1 cup (120g) frozen peas
120g baby spinach leaves
1 tbsp thyme leaves, plus extra to serve
2 tsp finely grated lemon rind
2½ cups (250g) coarsely grated cheddar or pizza cheese
¼ cup (20g) finely grated parmesan
½ cup (35g) panko (Japanese) breadcrumbs

Preheat oven to 240°C/220°C fan-forced. Grease a 2.5-litre (10-cup) ovenproof dish.

Place cauliflower on a large oven tray, drizzle with oil and season; toss to coat well. Roast for 15 mins or until almost tender and browned. Reduce oven to 220°C/200°C fan-forced

Meanwhile, cook pasta in a large saucepan of salted boiling water for 2 mins less than packet directions so it's firmer than al dente (which means there should be a little resistance when you bite into it). Drain.

Heat sour cream and buttermilk in a large heavy-based saucepan over low heat. Stir in peas, spinach, thyme, half the lemon rind and three-quarters of the combined cheeses; stir until well combined. Season.

Combine remaining cheeses, lemon rind and the breadcrumbs in a small bowl.

Stir pasta into hot cheese sauce; spoon evenly into dish. Press cauliflower pieces into pasta mixture. Sprinkle with breadcrumb mixture.

Bake for 20 mins or until crumbs are browned and mixture is heated through. Serve with extra thyme.

MID-WEEK WINNER

Drum roll please! Introducing the drumette

PREP + COOK TIME 45 MINUTES

DID YOU KNOW THE DRUMETTE IS THE FIRST JOINT OF THE WING? NOW WINGS ARE NOT MY HUSBAND'S FAVE, BUT THIS IS A GOOD WAY TO FEED MY MAN CHICKEN!

SERVES 4

2 tbsp tandoori paste
1½ cups (420g) Greek yoghurt
1kg chicken drumettes
1 Lebanese cucumber
1 tbsp mint leaves
1 tbsp lemon juice
halved cherry tomatoes, lemon wedges and warmed Indian flatbreads, to serve

Preheat oven to 200°C/180°C fan-forced. Line a large oven tray with baking paper.

Place tandoori paste and half the yoghurt in a large bowl (reserve remaining yoghurt for raita). Season with salt and pepper. Mix well to combine. Add chicken to bowl and mix until well coated. Place coated chicken in neat rows on tray.

Bake chicken for 30 mins or until golden brown and cooked through.

Meanwhile, to make raita, coarsely grate cucumber and place in a colander. Using clean hands, squeeze out as much liquid as possible. Coarsely chop mint. Place reserved yoghurt in a bowl. Add lemon juice and season with salt; stir to combine. Top yoghurt mixture with cucumber and mint. Cover bowl and refrigerate until needed.

When ready to serve, stir the cucumber and mint into the yoghurt. Serve chicken with raita, tomatoes, lemon wedges and warmed flatbreads.

BARELY ANY PREP

Teriyaki salmon

PREP + COOK TIME 35 MINUTES (+ REFRIGERATION)

THE KIND OF MEAL YOU'LL ORDER AT A JAPANESE RESTAURANT. BUT NOW YOU CAN MAKE IT AT HOME! TASTY, HEALTHY, WITH PLENTY OF WOW FACTOR.

SERVES 4

¼ cup (60ml) soy sauce
¼ cup (90g) honey
1 tbsp grated fresh ginger or ginger paste
1 tbsp lime juice
600g piece skinless salmon fillet
500g microwave brown rice
200g frozen shelled edamame (soya beans)
1 telegraph cucumber, sliced thinly lengthways into ribbons (see tip)
2 tbsp lemon juice
2 tsp sesame oil
1 green onion, shredded
2 tsp sesame seeds, toasted

To make the teriyaki marinade, combine the soy sauce, honey, ginger and lime juice in a small bowl. Place salmon in a shallow ovenproof dish; pour over marinade. Turn salmon to coat; refrigerate for at least 30 mins.

Preheat oven to 200°C/180°C fan-forced. Line an oven tray with baking paper.

Meanwhile, warm rice according to packet directions.

Boil, steam or microwave the edamame until warmed though; cool slightly.

Place salmon on lined tray; roast for 15 mins or until cooked to your liking. Transfer the salmon to a plate, cover loosely with foil; rest for 5 mins.

Meanwhile, strain the roasting juices into a small saucepan; bring to the boil over medium-high heat. Boil for 5 mins or until sauce is thickened slightly.

Combine rice, cucumber, edamame, lemon juice and sesame oil in a large bowl.

Serve teriyaki salmon with rice salad, drizzle with teriyaki sauce and sprinkle with green onion and sesame seeds.

TIP Use a vegetable peeler to thinly slice the cucumber lengthways.

BARELY ANY PREP

Delish Japanese pancake (*okonomiyaki*)

PREP + COOK TIME 25 MINUTES

OKONOMIYAKI – MEANING 'WHAT YOU LIKE' – IS A DELICIOUS PANCAKE USING TOPPINGS FOR TEXTURE AND FLAVOUR. IT'S ALSO A WAY TO USE UP ANY LEFTOVERS FROM THE FRIDGE. USUALLY I DON'T KNOW WHAT TO DO WITH CABBAGE BUT HERE IT WON'T BE OUT OF PLACE!

SERVES 4

2 medium zucchini
1 small carrot
¾ cup (110g) plain flour
3 eggs, beaten lightly
3 cups (240g) white shredded cabbage
6 green onions, sliced thinly
1½ tbsp vegetable oil
2 x 30g Tokyo chicken-flavoured ramen noodles
6 slices streaky bacon (180g), trimmed to fit pan
¼ cup (70g) tomato sauce
1 tbsp Worcestershire sauce
1 tbsp oyster sauce
2 tsp caster sugar
Japanese mayonnaise (Kewpie) and lemon wedges, to serve

Preheat grill to high heat.

Coarsely grate the zucchini and carrot into a bowl; using your hands, squeeze out excess liquid.

Whisk flour, egg and ¾ cup (180ml) water in a bowl until smooth. Add zucchini, carrot, half the cabbage and half the green onion to egg mixture; season, mix to combine.

Heat oil in a 26cm non-stick or cast-iron ovenproof frying pan over medium-high heat. Add the pancake mixture; spread evenly in pan, scatter with ramen noodles, crushing them with your hand. Cook for 4 mins or until golden on the base. Place bacon over the top; transfer pan to the grill. Cook for 8 mins or until golden and cooked through.

Meanwhile, whisk sauces and sugar in a small bowl.

Slide pancake onto a plate. Drizzle with the sauce mixture and mayonnaise; top with the remaining cabbage and green onion. Serve with lemon wedges.

MID-WEEK WINNER

Restful pumpkin & chicken risotto

PREP + COOK TIME 1 HOUR

USUALLY THERE'S NOTHING RESTFUL ABOUT MAKING RISOTTO. FORGET EVERYTHING YOU KNOW ABOUT THIS TRADITIONALLY TRICKY DISH – THIS VERSION HAS ALMOST NO STIRRING!

SERVES 4-6

500g butternut pumpkin, peeled, cut into 2cm pieces
1 tbsp finely chopped rosemary
2 tbsp extra virgin olive oil
1 onion, chopped finely
2 cloves garlic, crushed
1¼ cups (250g) arborio rice
½ cup (125ml) dry white wine
2 chicken stock cubes
2 cups (320g) thickly shredded cooked chicken
75g baby spinach leaves
1 cup (80g) freshly grated parmesan
2 tsp finely grated lemon rind

Preheat oven to 200°C/180°C fan-forced. Line an oven tray with baking paper.

Place pumpkin on tray. Sprinkle with half the rosemary and drizzle with half the oil. Bake for 25 mins or until golden and tender.

Meanwhile, heat remaining oil in a large, heavy-based flameproof and ovenproof dish over medium heat. Add onion and garlic; cook, stirring, for 5 mins or until onion is soft.

Add the rice, stir for 1 min until rice is coated. Add wine, 3½ cups (875ml) water and crumbled stock cubes. Bring to the boil. Cover dish with foil.

Bake for 20 mins or until liquid is almost absorbed, stirring chicken into rice during the last 5 mins.

Coarsely shred half the spinach, stir into risotto. Add three-quarters of the parmesan, half the lemon rind and most of the pumpkin. Serve topped with remaining pumpkin and rosemary, whole spinach leaves, rind and parmesan. Season with pepper.

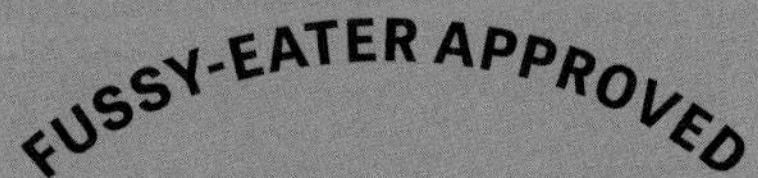

Winner, winner, chicken dinner

PREP + COOK TIME 1 HOUR 20 MINUTES

ROAST CHOOK SEEMED TOO HARD UNTIL MY BFF DENISE DRYSDALE SHOWED ME HOW TO COOK IT. BUT I STILL USE GRAVY FROM A PACKET.

SERVES 4

2 tbsp olive oil
1 clove garlic, bruised
1.6kg chicken
1 medium lemon (140g), quartered
4 sprigs fresh thyme, plus extra to serve
2 cups (500ml) chicken stock
6 desiree potatoes, peeled
2 tsp chicken salt
165g ready-made gravy, warmed

Preheat oven to 200°C/180°C fan-forced. Combine oil and garlic in a small bowl. Pat chicken dry with paper towel. Tuck wings under body. Brush chicken with half the garlic-infused oil. Fill chicken cavity with lemon and thyme sprigs; season. Tie legs together with kitchen string.

Place chicken on a rack in a roasting pan. Pour stock into pan without wetting chicken. Roast for 15 mins.

Meanwhile, cut potatoes in half lengthways, then cut each half into three wedges (the increased surface area means more crisp bits). Cook potatoes in a saucepan of boiling water for 10 mins or until almost tender. Drain; stand in a colander to air dry.

Reduce oven to 180°C/160°C fan-forced; roast chicken a further 45 mins or until cooked through. When the chicken has 20 mins cooking time remaining, place potatoes in a roasting pan, drizzle with remaining garlic oil and sprinkle with half the chicken salt; place potatoes in oven with chicken.

Remove chicken from oven. Transfer to a plate; cover loosely with foil. Increase oven to the highest setting; roast potatoes a further 10 mins or until golden.

Serve chicken and potatoes with gravy; sprinkle with remaining chicken salt (or sea salt flakes if you're feeling fancy) and extra thyme.

MID-WEEK WINNER

Chicken parmi bake

PREP + COOK TIME 50 MINUTES

JUST A FEW OF MY FAVOURITE THINGS HERE – SAUCE IN A JAR, CHEESE AND EVERYTHING COOKED IN ONE DISH. AND DON'T STRESS IF THE GREENS GET OVERLOOKED.

SERVES 4

3 cups (750ml) tomato pasta sauce
2 tbsp tomato paste
600g chicken breast fillets, quartered lengthways
1 bunch broccolini, each cut into thirds
2 medium zucchini, sliced thinly
220g bocconcini, sliced
3 cups (210g) coarsely torn sourdough bread
2 tsp fennel seeds
2 tbsp extra virgin olive oil
½ cup (40g) finely grated parmesan
coarsely chopped parsley leaves, to serve

Preheat oven to 180°C/160°C fan-forced.

Lightly grease a 2.5-litre (10-cup) rectangular ovenproof dish. Combine pasta sauce and tomato paste; spoon half the sauce mixture over base of dish. Top with chicken and vegies. Spoon over remaining sauce and top with bocconcini.

Combine the torn bread, fennel seeds, oil and parmesan in a small bowl, season; scatter over chicken mixture.

Bake for 30 mins or until the top is browned lightly and chicken is cooked through. Serve immediately, sprinkled with parsley leaves.

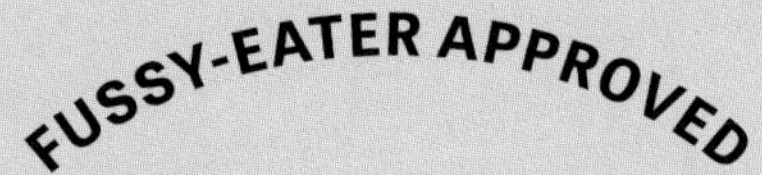

Bestest, baddest, biggest burgers

PREP + COOK TIME 30 MINUTES

FRIENDS MIGHT THINK YOU'RE OPENING UP YOUR OWN BURGER SHOP WITH THESE BEAUTIES. AND IF IT'S ALL TOO HARD I BUY MY MEAT PATTIES FROM THE BUTCHER.

MAKES 4

1 tbsp brown sugar
2 tbsp soy sauce
2 tbsp gochujang chilli paste (see tip)
2 cloves garlic, crushed
2 tsp finely grated ginger
800g beef mince
1 egg
¾ cup (75g) breadcrumbs
2 tbsp barbecue sauce
2 tbsp olive oil
4 large burger buns (400g)
4 slices burger cheese or cheddar (160g)
2 cups (160g) store-bought kale slaw
⅓ cup (100g) mayonnaise

Combine sugar, soy sauce, chilli paste, garlic and ginger in a bowl. Add beef, egg and breadcrumbs; using your hands, combine well. Shape mixture into four patties (make sure they are the same size as the burger buns). Brush all over with barbecue sauce.

Heat oil in a large non-stick frying pan over medium heat. Add the patties; cook for 6 mins each side or until browned and cooked through. Remove from pan and keep warm.

Wipe pan clean and return to heat. Split buns then cook, cut-side down, for 30 secs. Turn over and add a slice of cheese to the bases. Reduce heat to low; cover with a lid; cook for 1 min or until cheese melts.

Layer bun bases with patties, slaw and mayonnaise; sandwich together with bun tops.

TIP Gochujang is a Korean fermented red chilli paste, available in major supermarkets.

MID-WEEK WINNER

Carbonara my way

PREP + COOK TIME 25 MINUTES

APOLOGIES IN ADVANCE TO MY ITALIAN FRIENDS – I KNOW TRADITIONALLY CARBONARA DOESN'T HAVE CREAM BUT I LOVE THIS CREAMIER AND CHEESIER VERSION. WHEN IN ROME, WITH MY MUM AND SISTERS, I INSISTED ON WEARING A GLADIATOR HELMET AND ORDERED CARBONARA EVERY NIGHT. AND THIS DISH REMINDS ME OF OUR ROMA ADVENTURE!

SERVES 4

100g pancetta, chopped finely
2 cloves garlic, crushed
1 cup (250ml) pouring cream
375g dried linguine
4 eggs, beaten lightly
1 cup (80g) finely grated parmesan, plus extra to serve
2 tbsp finely chopped flat-leaf parsley

Bring a large saucepan of generously salted water to the boil.

Cook the pancetta in a large non-stick frying pan for 5 mins or until starting to crisp (you don't need to add oil to the pan). Add garlic; cook, stirring, for 1 min. Add cream and bring to a simmer; simmer for 4 mins or until thickened.

Meanwhile, add pasta to boiling water; cook for 10 mins or until al dente (until there's still a little resistance when you bite into it). Remove ½ cup cooking water, then drain pasta.

Combine egg, parmesan and pasta cooking water in a large jug. Add pasta to the pan, toss to coat in cream mixture, then add egg mixture; stir over medium heat for 1 min or until well combined (don't overcook or the egg will scramble). Stir in parsley; season with pepper and serve with extra parmesan.

CAN'T BE BOTHERED You could use 4 finely chopped rindless bacon slices (260g) instead of pancetta and 1 tsp garlic paste instead of fresh garlic (I usually do!).

MAGIC MINCE

Chilli con carne pie

PREP + COOK TIME 1 HOUR

FORGET TEA AND SCONES – THIS FAMILY FRIENDLY DISH IS ALL ABOUT CORN AND SCONES, AND MINCE PLAYS A STARRING ROLE IN THIS REIMAGINED CHILLI CON CARNE.

SERVES 6

2 tbsp extra virgin olive oil
1 onion, sliced thinly
1 red capsicum, seeded, sliced thinly
2 cloves garlic, crushed
2 tsp chilli powder or sweet paprika
2 tsp ground cumin
1 tsp dried oregano
750g beef mince
2 x 400g cans diced tomatoes
1 cup (250ml) vegetable stock
2 x 400g cans four-bean mix, drained, rinsed
460g savoury cheese & chive scone mix
125g can corn kernels, drained
coriander leaves and salad, to serve

Heat half the oil in a large heavy-based saucepan over medium-high heat; cook onion, capsicum and garlic, stirring, for 5 mins or until onion softens. Add chilli, cumin and oregano; cook, stirring, for 1 min or until fragrant. Add beef; cook, stirring with a wooden spoon to break up any lumps, for 5 mins or until browned. Add tomatoes, stock and bean mix; bring to the boil. Reduce heat to low-medium; simmer for 20 mins or until sauce thickens slightly. Season to taste.

Meanwhile, preheat oven to 200°C/180°C fan-forced. Combine the scone mix and half the corn in a bowl; add ¾ cup (180ml) water, stir to form a sticky dough.

Spoon beef mixture into a 2-litre (8-cup) ovenproof frying pan or ovenproof dish. Drop tablespoons of corn scone dough on top of beef mixture, brush with remaining oil and top with remaining corn. Bake for 20 mins or until browned.

Top the pie with coriander (and sea salt flakes, if you're feeling fancy). Serve with salad.

NO-CUTLERY NACHOS

RECIPE PAGES 70 & 71

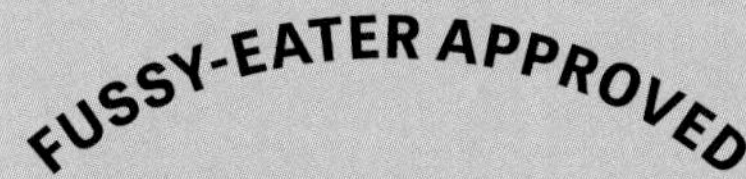

No-cutlery nachos

PREP + COOK TIME 45 MINUTES

NACHOS IS AT THE TOP OF MY FOOD CHAIN. SO MUCH SO, I'VE EVEN MADE MYSELF A NACHOS HAT TO WEAR WHEN I PREPARE THIS FEAST. WHAT I LOVE ABOUT IT IS THE SIMPLICITY. THERE'S PLENTY OF CUPBOARD STAPLES INCLUDING CANS OF BEANS, TOMATOES, PASTA SAUCE AND CORN CHIPS.

HOWEVER, PLEASE DON'T MAKE THE MISTAKE I DID AND USE BAKING PAPER WITH THE CORN CHIPS AND CHEESE. NOT SURPRISINGLY I GOT DISTRACTED TALKING AND IT CAUGHT FIRE UNDER THE GRILL! STICK WITH THE FOIL!

THE BEAUTY HERE IS YOU CAN SERVE THE NACHOS STRAIGHT ONTO YOUR BENCH TOP OR TABLE – AND I'D LIKE TO THINK YOU'RE WEARING A NACHOS HAT TOO!

SERVES 8-10

2 tbsp extra virgin olive oil
600g beef mince
2 cloves garlic, crushed
1 tsp ground cumin
1 tsp ground coriander
400g can diced tomatoes
400g jar Arrabbiata pasta sauce
250g cherry tomatoes, quartered
2 tbsp lime juice
2 avocados, halved, stone removed
400g can kidney beans, drained, rinsed
400g can black beans, drained, rinsed
2 x 200g packets corn chips
1 cup (100g) shredded pizza cheese
280g jar nacho cheese salsa (see tip)
½ cup coriander leaves
lime wedges, to serve

Preheat oven to 180°C/160°C fan-forced. Line two large oven trays and your dining table with foil.

Heat oil in a large frying pan over medium heat. Add the beef; cook for 5 mins, stirring with a wooden spoon to break up any lumps, until beef is browned.

Add garlic and spices; stir for 1 min or until fragrant. Add canned tomatoes and pasta sauce to pan. Stir to combine. Bring to the boil, then reduce heat. Simmer for 5 mins.

Meanwhile, combine tomatoes and half the lime juice in a small bowl; season to taste.

Scoop avocado flesh into a second small bowl, add remaining lime juice and season, then crush with a fork.

Add beans to the beef mixture in pan. Cook for a further 3 mins, stirring occasionally, until beef mixture is thickened slightly. Lightly mash some of the beans in the pan with the back of a fork or a potato masher.

Meanwhile, arrange corn chips on oven trays overlapping slightly; scatter with cheese, bake for 5 mins or until cheese is melted and chips are warmed.

Slide chips onto foil-lined table. Spoon the beef mixture over corn chips. Top with the tomato mixture, mashed avocado, cheese salsa and coriander leaves. Season with pepper. Serve with lime wedges.

TIP Nacho cheese salsa is available in supermarkets.

Sugar

Can't Be Bothered – Dinners Made Easy

MAGIC MINCE

One-pan chicken san choy bau

PREP + COOK TIME 25 MINUTES

ANOTHER DELIGHT FROM THE EVER-VERSATILE MINCE, AND DEPENDING ON THE PRICE OF LETTUCE YOU CAN ALWAYS LEAVE IT OUT!

SERVES 4

1 tbsp vegetable oil
2 cloves garlic, crushed
600g chicken mince
⅓ cup (90g) grated palm sugar
2 tbsp fish sauce
1 tbsp lemongrass paste
½ cup (40g) fried shallots, plus extra to serve
⅓ cup (45g) chopped roasted peanuts
200g microwave jasmine rice
1 tbsp lime juice
1 cup coriander or Thai basil leaves
2 baby cos lettuce, leaves separated
1 long red or green chilli, sliced thinly
lime wedges, to serve

Heat oil in a wok over high heat; stir-fry garlic and chicken for 5 mins or until chicken is browned.

Add sugar, fish sauce, lemongrass, fried shallots and chopped peanuts to wok. Reduce heat to low; stir-fry for 2 mins or until mixture is sticky. Add rice; toss for 3 mins or until heated through.

Remove from heat; add lime juice and three-quarters of the coriander.

Spoon mince mixture into lettuce leaves; top with chilli, extra fried shallots and the remaining coriander. (If you want even more crunch, add some extra chopped peanuts too.) Serve with lime wedges.

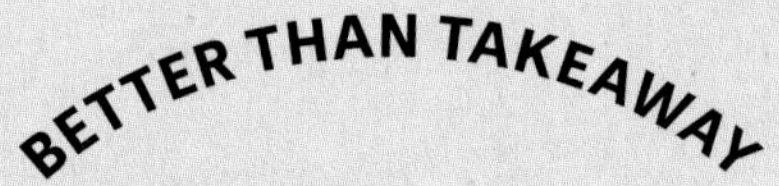

Bowl-me-over burrito

PREP + COOK TIME 40 MINUTES

YOU'LL NEVER LOOK AT A BURRITO THE SAME WAY AGAIN. NO NEED FOR WRAPPING (I'VE BEEN KNOWN TO USE RUBBER BANDS!).

SERVES 4

- **8 x 20cm wholemeal tortillas**
- **olive oil cooking spray**
- **2 tbsp extra virgin olive oil**
- **1 onion, sliced thinly**
- **500g mince of your choice (beef, chicken or pork)**
- **30g sachet taco spice mix**
- **400g can kidney beans, drained, rinsed**
- **400g can crushed tomatoes**
- **2 baby cos lettuce, leaves separated**
- **1 medium avocado, diced**
- **2 tbsp lime juice**
- **1 cup (120g) grated cheddar**
- **sour cream, shredded green onion, hot sauce and lime wedges, to serve**

Preheat oven to 180°C/160°C fan-forced. Place eight large ramekins onto an oven tray (see tip).

Spray tortillas with cooking oil spray. Press tortillas, oil-side down, into bowls to create basket shapes. Spray with a little more cooking oil spray.

Bake tortillas for 10 mins or until lightly browned. Remove tray from oven. Leave tortillas in bowls to cool.

Heat olive oil in a large non-stick frying pan over medium heat. Add onion; cook, stirring occasionally, for 5 mins or until soft. Increase heat to high. Add mince to pan; cook, stirring with a wooden spoon to break up any lumps, for 5 mins or until browned. Sprinkle spice mix over mince mixture. Cook for a further 2 mins or until fragrant.

Add beans and tomatoes to the pan; cook, stirring occasionally, for 10 mins or until the mince mixture thickens. Season to taste.

Remove tortillas from bowls. Divide lettuce, mince mixture and combined avocado and lime juice among tortilla bowls. Top with sour cream, cheese, green onion and hot sauce. Serve with lime wedges.

TIP If you don't have eight large ramekins, work with four instead and repeat the cooking process.

MID-WEEK WINNER

Triumphant one-pan gnocchi

PREP + COOK TIME 15 MINUTES

THREE OF MY HERO INGREDIENTS IN ONE PAN – PASTA, CREAM AND MUSHIES. YES, I DO HAVE DAUGHTERS WHO PICK OUT THE MUSHROOMS WHICH JUST MEANS THERE'S MORE FOR ME AND PETEE, MY HUSBAND.

SERVES 4

625g fresh potato gnocchi
40g butter
400g assorted mushrooms, whole or sliced
2 cloves garlic, crushed
300ml pouring cream
90g baby spinach leaves, trimmed
⅔ cup (50g) finely grated parmesan

Place the gnocchi in a large frying pan with enough boiling water from the kettle to cover. Bring to the boil over medium heat; cook for 4 minutes or until heated through. Drain and keep warm.

Dry frying pan and place over medium-high heat. Add butter; when butter is melted, add mushrooms, cook, stirring occasionally, for 4 mins or until softened and golden. Stir in garlic; cook for 2 mins.

Add cream; bring to the boil. Reduce heat to low; simmer for 3 mins or until sauce thickens. Stir in spinach and half the parmesan. Season to taste.

Add the gnocchi to pan; stir gently to combine. Top gnocchi with remaining parmesan; season with pepper to serve.

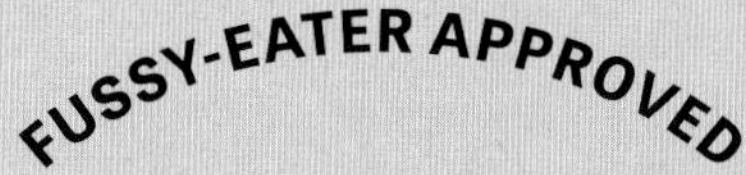

Easy-peasy pizza loaf

PREP + COOK TIME 25 MINUTES

PIZZA IS ONE OF THE MAJOR FOOD GROUPS IN OUR HOUSEHOLD. THIS LOAF IS SO MUCH FASTER TO MAKE THAN PIZZA, JUST AS TASTY AND QUICKER THAN HOME DELIVERY! AND OF COURSE I HAVE A PIZZA HAT TO MATCH THIS MEAL.

SERVES 6

1 cobb loaf (400g)
½ cup (140g) pizza sauce
2 cloves garlic, crushed
1 tbsp extra virgin olive oil
1 cup (100g) grated mozzarella
½ cup (60g) sliced pitted green olives
basil leaves, to serve

Preheat oven to 180°C/160°C fan-forced. Line an oven tray with baking paper.

Using a serrated knife, make cuts into cobb loaf, 2cm apart, three-quarters of the way through; repeat in the other direction to form a cross-hatch pattern. Place on lined tray.

Combine pizza sauce, garlic and oil in a small bowl. Divide sauce mixture and mozzarella evenly into each cut. Press in the olives.

Bake pizza loaf for 15 mins or until cheese is melted and bread is golden and crisp. Top with basil.

TIP For meat-lovers, add salami, ham or pepperoni (or all three) before baking.

BARELY ANY PREP

BLT salad with chook

PREP + COOK TIME 20 MINUTES

I TREAT MYSELF TO A BLT IF I GET A NIGHT AWAY TO MYSELF. COOK THIS UP AND IMAGINE YOU'VE ORDERED ROOM SERVICE.

SERVES 4

olive oil cooking spray
8 rindless bacon slices (520g)
1 tsp smoked paprika
1 tbsp olive oil
12 chicken tenderloins (900g)
2 tsp Dijon mustard
1 tbsp lemon juice
⅔ cup (190g) Greek yoghurt
1 clove garlic, crushed
2 baby cos lettuce, trimmed, leaves separated
250g cherry or grape tomatoes, halved
2 eschalots, sliced finely

Spray a medium frying pan with cooking oil spray; place over medium heat, cook bacon, turning, for 3 mins or until crisp. Drain on paper towel, then tear into large pieces.

Combine paprika, oil and chicken in a small bowl. Season.

Heat same pan over medium-high heat; cook chicken for 2 mins each side or until cooked through.

Stir mustard, lemon juice, yoghurt, garlic and 1 tbsp water in a small bowl.

Layer lettuce, bacon, chicken, tomatoes and eschalots in a shallow bowl; drizzle with yoghurt dressing.

TIP You could also use a store-bought BBQ chicken and pull the meat off the bones in large pieces.

BARELY ANY PREP

Couch baked bean & cheddar jaffles

PREP + COOK TIME 10 MINUTES

BAKED BEANS IS OUR SUNDAY NIGHT MEAL AS PETEE IS ALWAYS WORKING THAT NIGHT AND BEANS AREN'T TOP OF HIS LIST. FOR ME, NOTHING BEATS THE COMFORT OF A TOASTED SANDWICH WITH MELTED CHEESE EATEN IN FRONT OF THE TELLY TO PREPARE FOR THE BUSY WEEK AHEAD.

SERVES 2

60g butter, softened
8 slices white bread
⅓ cup (110g) tomato relish
300g can baked beans
⅔ cup (80g) grated cheddar
curly parsley, to serve (optional)

Preheat jaffle iron, sandwich press or frying pan.

Butter both sides of bread with softened butter. Spread half the bread slices with tomato relish. Top with baked beans and grated cheddar; season. Top with remaining bread.

Toast for 3 mins or until golden and crisp (if using a frying pan, cook for 3 mins each side). Serve topped with parsley, if using.

TIPS The filling combos are as endless as your imagination. Fresh air can be breathed into leftover spaghetti Bolognese, roast vegies or meat with the help of a condiment and/or cheese. You can easily increase the ingredient quantities as needed to serve more people.

MID-WEEK WINNER

Tex-Mex-Aus brisket tostadas

PREP + COOK TIME 45 MINUTES

NEVER UNDERESTIMATE THE VERSATILITY OF A TORTILLA! AND DON'T MAKE MY PAST MISTAKE OF NOT WEARING YOUR READING GLASSES WHILE CHECKING THE HEATING INSTRUCTIONS. MINE WENT FROM CRISPY TO CHARCOAL!

SERVES 4

700g packaged slow-cooked beef brisket
2 corn cobs, husks and silks removed
¼ cup (60ml) extra virgin olive oil
12 mini tortillas or shells, warmed
250g mixed cherry tomatoes, halved
1 Lebanese cucumber, diced finely
⅓ cup coriander leaves
1 tbsp lime juice
1 baby cos lettuce, leaves separated
220g store-bought guacamole
lime wedges, to serve

Preheat oven to 200°C/180°C fan-forced. Line a small oven tray with baking paper.

Remove beef from packaging, place on lined tray; cook on the lower shelf of the oven for 25 mins, turning halfway through, until caramelised and heated through.

Meanwhile, place corn on a large oven tray; rub with 1 tbsp of the oil, season. Place corn on the top shelf of the oven near the element; cook for 10 mins or until cooked and lightly browned. When cool enough to handle, use a sharp knife to cut corn kernels from cobs, in sections if possible. Reserve tray.

Stack tortillas and wrap in foil, place on reserved tray; bake for 10 mins or until warmed through.

Combine tomatoes, cucumber, corn kernels and coriander in a bowl. Whisk remaining oil and the lime juice in a small jug; season. Pour dressing over the tomato mixture; toss gently to coat.

Using two forks, shred meat on tray. Serve shredded meat, corn salad, lettuce, guacamole and lime wedges in separate bowls with serving utensils for people to pile onto their own tostadas.

ONE-POT WONDER

One-pot Bolognese saviour

PREP + COOK TIME 30 MINUTES

SPAG BOL HAS FUELLED MY FAMILY SINCE THE BEGINNING OF TIME. IT'S SOMETHING I'VE ALWAYS 'COOKED' AND MY GIRLS TELL ME I SHOULD BE ON MASTERCHEF WITH THIS MEAL. THIS MEAL CAN BE REIMAGINED FOR SCHOOL LUNCHBOXES, REHEATED FOR ANOTHER NIGHT – ITS USES ARE ENDLESS.

SERVES 4

1 tbsp extra virgin olive oil
1 onion, chopped coarsely
3 cloves garlic, crushed
500g beef mince
½ tsp dried chilli flakes
3 cups (780g) bottled tomato pasta sauce
400g penne pasta
2 cups (240g) coarsely grated cheddar
½ cup (40g) grated parmesan
flat-leaf parsley leaves, to serve (optional)

Heat oil in a large saucepan over high heat; cook onion, garlic, beef and chilli, stirring, for 6 mins or until beef is browned.

Stir in sauce; simmer for 2 mins. Add 3 cups (750ml) boiling water and the uncooked pasta; bring to the boil. Simmer, covered, stirring occasionally, for 20 mins or until pasta is tender.

Stir in 1½ cups cheddar; season to taste. Sprinkle pasta with remaining cheddar, the parmesan and parsley, if using.

TIP To add some hidden vegies, add a little coarsely grated zucchini, finely grated carrot and quartered mushrooms after browning the beef.

MID-WEEK WINNER

Not soggy stir-fry

PREP + COOK TIME 35 MINUTES (+ STANDING)

CHEF GENIUS ADAM LIAW TAUGHT ME NOT TO CROWD THE WOK WITH TOO MANY DIFFERENT TYPES OF VEGIES. KEEP IT SIMPLE AND NO MORE SOGGINESS!

SERVES 4

2 tbsp light soy sauce
1 tbsp Shaoxing
1 tsp sea salt flakes
1 tsp white sugar
600g protein of your choice (chicken breast, beef or pork fillet)
200g crunchy vegies of your choice (celery, carrot, baby corn, capsicum)
200g green vegies of your choice (snow peas, gai lan, broccolini, broccoli)
¼ cup (60ml) vegetable oil
1 tsp ginger paste
1 tsp garlic paste
4 green onions, sliced
1 tsp sesame oil
steamed rice, to serve
toppings of your choice, to serve (crushed wasabi peas, fried shallots; optional)

Combine 1 tbsp of the soy sauce, the Shaoxing, salt and sugar in a bowl. Cut your chosen protein thickly on the diagonal; add to the marinade and turn to coat. Set aside while preparing the vegies.

Thinly slice the crunchy vegies, if using corn, halve lengthways. For green vegies, keep snow peas whole unless large. If using gai lan or broccolini cut into 4cm lengths, keeping the stalks and top parts separate. Cut broccoli into florets.

Heat 1 tbsp oil in a wok or large heavy-based frying pan; stir-fry crunchy vegies for 3 mins or until just tender. Add remaining 1 tbsp soy sauce; transfer to a large plate.

Rinse wok; wipe clean. Heat another 1 tbsp of the oil in wok over high heat; add protein of choice. Stir-fry for 8 mins or until browned and cooked through. Transfer to a bowl.

Add the remaining oil to wok, add green vegies of choice (reserving tops, if using gai lan or broccolini), the ginger, garlic and green onion; stir fry for 2 mins (adding vegie tops halfway through) or until just tender. Return protein and crunchy veg to wok with sesame oil; stir to combine.

Serve stir-fry with steamed rice and scatter with any topping ingredients you like.

LAZY MODE

Emergency smoothies

STAY COOL WITH THESE SENSATIONAL SMOOTHIES. FREEZING THE FRUIT IS ALSO AN UNREAL BANANA PEEL WAY OF NOT WASTING THOSE BROWN BANANAS IN YOUR FRUIT BOWL. DECORATING THE GLASSES MIGHT TEMPT YOUR KIDS TO 'DRINK' SOME FRUIT.

BANANA IS A-GO-GO

PREP TIME 10 MINUTES (+ FREEZING)
MAKES 2

Peel and chop 1 large banana. Place in a zip-lock plastic bag. Freeze for 3 hours or until firm. Place banana, 2 cups frozen strawberries, 1 cup (250ml) milk, ½ cup thick Greek yoghurt and 2 tsp honey into a blender or food processor. Blend on high speed until smooth. Divide between glasses.

FLAVOUR TWIST Blend in 1-2 tbsp peanut butter for a PB&J version, or 1-2 tbsp malted milk for a malt version.

SUMMERTIME RESCUE

PREP TIME 10 MINUTES
MAKES 2

Peel and core half a small pineapple; chop into small pieces. Place the pineapple, 1 cup frozen raspberries, ½ cup frozen mango pieces and 1 cup (250ml) chilled Coco Quench (coconut and rice milk blend) in a blender or food processor. Blend on high speed until smooth. Divide between glasses. Serve with pineapple wedges, if you like.

FLAVOUR TWIST Blend in 1-2 tbsp almond butter. For an adult version, add a little rum!

FRIDGE SWEEP

Friday fridge fried rice

PREP + COOK TIME 25 MINUTES

EVERYONE LOVES FRIED RICE! KEEP IT SIMPLE WITH MICROWAVE RICE AND USE WHATEVER LEFTOVERS YOU HAVE IN THE FRIDGE. THE EGG MAKES IT RESTAURANT-STYLE.

SERVES 4

- **2 tbsp vegetable oil**
- **2 eggs, beaten lightly**
- **¼ cup (80g) tom yum paste (see tips)**
- **5 chicken thigh fillets (850g), sliced thinly**
- **1 red capsicum, sliced thinly**
- **1 red onion, sliced thinly**
- **2 cups shredded cabbage**
- **½ cup (60g) frozen peas, thawed**
- **150g oyster mushrooms, torn**
- **1 tsp garlic paste**
- **2 x 250g packets microwave white basmati rice**
- **2 green onions, sliced thinly**
- **soy sauce, to taste**

Heat 1 tsp of the vegetable oil in a large wok over high heat. Pour egg into wok; swirl wok so egg coats the base, cook 2 mins or until omelette is just set. Remove omelette from wok; chop coarsely.

Heat 3 tsp of the remaining oil in wok; add tom yum paste, stir-fry over high heat for 3 mins or until fragrant. Add chicken; stir-fry for 4 mins or until browned and cooked through. Remove from wok.

Heat remaining oil in wok; stir-fry capsicum, red onion, cabbage, peas, mushrooms and garlic for 3 mins or until vegies soften.

Return chicken and egg to wok with rice and half the green onion; stir-fry until heated through. (Taste the fried rice and add soy sauce to taste.)

Serve rice sprinkled with remaining green onion.

TIPS Tom yum paste is the rockstar ingredient of this recipe, adding a big flavour note all in one ingredient. You could also use Thai red curry paste to similar effect. Replace capsicum, cabbage and mushrooms with other thinly sliced vegies from your fridge.

BARELY ANY PREP

Mum's Waldorf salad

PREP + COOK TIME 25 MINUTES (+ COOLING)

MUM MADE THIS SALAD FOR MY SISTERS AND I WHEN WE WERE GROWING UP. IT'S NAMED AFTER THE WALDORF ASTORIA HOTEL IN NEW YORK.

SERVES 4

3 chicken breast fillets (600g)
½ cup (150g) whole-egg mayonnaise
2 tbsp Dijon mustard
⅓ cup (80ml) lemon juice
2 red apples, sliced thinly
2 stalks celery, sliced thinly
1 small red onion, sliced thinly
4 handfuls of salad lettuce of your choice
300g red grapes, halved
1 cup (100g) walnuts, roasted

Place chicken in a small saucepan with enough water to cover; bring to the boil. Reduce heat to low-medium; cook for 7 mins or until just cooked through. Cool in poaching liquid. When cool enough to handle, shred thickly.

Meanwhile, to make the Dijon mayonnaise dressing. place mayonnaise, mustard and ¼ cup (60ml) of the lemon juice in a screw-top jar; season to taste. Shake well to combine.

Place apple and remaining lemon juice in a large bowl; toss to coat. Add shredded chicken, celery, onion, salad leaf of choice, grapes, walnuts and half the dressing; toss salad gently to combine. Season to taste.

Serve salad on a large platter drizzled with the remaining dressing.

CAN'T BE BOTHERED Pick a bag of your favourite salad leaf mix, or for more crunch choose iceberg or cos lettuce and tear into bite-sized pieces. You could also use leftover roast chicken or a store-bought BBQ chicken here.

MAGIC MINCE

Loaded microwave-to-grill spuds

PREP + COOK TIME 50 MINUTES

HELLO MINCE MY OLD FRIEND! HOW GOOD IS THIS TAKE ON MAKING A MEAL OUT OF A POTATO?! COMPLETE WITH SIMPLE MICROWAVE INSTRUCTIONS.

SERVES 4

1 tbsp extra virgin olive oil
1 small onion, chopped finely
1 tsp garlic paste
1 small carrot, chopped finely
1 small red capsicum, chopped finely
500g beef mince
1 tbsp mild American-style mustard
½ cup (140g) tomato sauce
⅓ cup (80ml) beef stock
6 small orange sweet potatoes, unpeeled
½ cup (50g) pizza cheese
finely chopped flat-leaf parsley, to serve

Heat oil in a large saucepan over medium-high heat; cook onion, garlic, carrot and capsicum, stirring, for 5 mins or until vegies soften. Increase heat to high, add beef; cook, stirring, for 5 mins or until browned.

Add mustard, sauce and stock to pan; cook, stirring, for 10 mins or until sauce thickens. Season.

Preheat grill to high. Line an oven tray with foil. Scrub sweet potatoes; pierce all over with a fork. Enclose each sweet potato separately in plastic wrap; microwave on HIGH for 10 mins or until tender. Cool for 5 mins; unwrap.

Make a 2cm deep cut, lengthways, into the top of each sweet potato. Using a tea towel, gently squeeze the base of each sweet potato to open the top. Place on the tray. Sprinkle sweet potatoes with half the cheese; grill for 3 mins or until cheese is melted.

Top potatoes with beef mixture and remaining cheese. Return to grill for 3 mins or until cheese is melted. Sprinkle with parsley and season with pepper.

FRIDGE SWEEP

Fridge hustle grazing board

PREP TIME 20 MINUTES

SINCE MY GIRLS HAVE BEEN TINY I'VE OFTEN PREPARED THEM A 'TASTING PLATE' OF CUT UP CARROTS, CHERRY TOMATOES AND AVOCADO WHICH THEY'LL EAT BEFORE DINNER. IT'S AN EASY WAY TO GET SOME VEGIES INTO THEM, AND MY MUM USED TO DO THE SAME FOR ME. THERE'S A TOUCH MORE EFFORT INVOLVED HERE BUT THE RESULT IS WORTH IT.

SERVES 4

130g store-bought chargrilled capsicum
200g store-bought hummus
1 tbsp taco spice mix
vegies of your choice (baby carrots, baby cucumbers, sugar snap peas, cherry tomatoes, celery sticks, avocado slices)
cheese of your choice (mini brie, bocconcini, cheddar)
crunchy things of your choice (grissini, pretzels, crackers, twists)

To make Mexican-spiced hummus, drain capsicum and pat dry with paper towel, then chop into small pieces. Place hummus, capsicum and spice mix in the bowl of a food processor or blender; process until smooth. Season to taste. Spoon hummus into a small bowl; sprinkle with paprika for a spicy kick, if you like.

Arrange remaining ingredients on a board or platter with the hummus in the centre for dipping.

TIP To make this even more substantial, serve with hard-boiled eggs: Place 4 room-temperature eggs in a small saucepan with enough cold water to just cover the eggs. Bring to the boil over high heat, then boil eggs for 5 mins. Remove eggs and cool under cold running water. Roll eggs on a work surface to crack the shell, then peel and halve.

BARELY ANY PREP

Sandwich press corn fritters

PREP + COOK TIME 30 MINUTES

YOU'RE MULTI-TASKING ALL THE TIME SO ISN'T IT A TREAT WHEN YOUR APPLIANCES CAN DO THE SAME! HERE IT'S THE SANDWICH PRESS AS ITS NON-STICK SURFACE IS A BRILLIANT HACK FOR COOKING FRITTERS. (WORKS WELL FOR PANCAKES AND PIKELETS, TOO.)

MAKES 18

1 cup frozen corn kernels
1 medium carrot
2 small zucchini
⅓ cup (30g) grated cheddar
2 eggs, beaten lightly
½ cup (90g) rice flour
1 tbsp extra virgin olive oil
Greek yoghurt, tomato relish and basil leaves, to serve

Place corn in a small bowl. Pour over enough boiling water from the kettle to cover. Stand for 1 min, then drain. Pat dry with paper towel.

Coarsely grate carrot and zucchini. Place grated zucchini in a colander. Using clean hands, squeeze out as much liquid as possible.

Place corn, carrot, zucchini, cheese, egg and rice flour in a bowl. Season with salt and pepper. Using a wooden spoon, mix until combined.

Preheat a flat-plated sandwich press. Lightly brush the top and bottom of the press with a little of the oil.

Working in batches, spoon heaped tablespoons of corn mixture onto the sandwich press, flattening the mixture slightly into rounds. Close the lid and cook for 2 mins or until fritters are golden brown. Transfer fritters to a plate and cover to keep warm. Repeat cooking with remaining corn mixture, lightly oiling the sandwich press in between batches, to make 18 fritters in total.

Serve fritters with yoghurt and tomato relish. Top with basil leaves (and sea salt flakes, if you're feeling fancy).

PINEAPPLE PASSION
Brewed Alcoholic
Seltzer
Dirty
Water
330ml
Dirty
Water

MID-WEEK WINNER

Say hello to awesome agnolotti

PREP + COOK TIME 30 MINUTES

SOMETIMES YOU NEED TO MIX UP YOUR PASTA ROUTINE. IT'S HARD FOR ME TO PUT THE PASTA SAUCE JAR ASIDE BUT I WILL FOR THIS RECIPE.

SERVES 4

8 slices prosciutto (120g)
500g packet pumpkin agnolotti
50g butter
1 medium leek, sliced thinly
2 cloves garlic, crushed
600g chicken tenderloins, cut into 6cm strips
½ cup (125ml) dry white wine
½ bunch sage, shredded, plus extra to serve
300ml thickened cream
2 medium zucchini, diced finely
1 lemon
2 tbsp grated parmesan

Preheat grill to high. Line an oven tray with baking paper.

Place prosciutto on lined tray; grill for 1 min on each side or until crisp.

Cook agnolotti in a large saucepan of salted boiling water following packet directions until just tender. Drain; return to pan to keep warm.

Meanwhile, melt butter in a large deep frying pan over medium heat; cook leek, stirring, for 5 mins or until softened and browned lightly.

Add garlic and chicken; cook, stirring occasionally, for 3 mins or until browned. Add wine; cook for 1 min or until almost evaporated. Add the sage, cream and zucchini, bring to the boil over high heat; cook for 2 mins or until chicken is cooked through.

Finely grate rind of lemon, then juice the lemon. Add pasta, lemon juice and parmesan to chicken mixture, season to taste; toss to combine.

Top pasta mixture with torn prosciutto, lemon rind and extra sage.

TIP You could also use 500g fresh fettuccine or ravioli instead of the agnolotti.

Sizzling sausage subs

PREP + COOK TIME 35 MINUTES

SAUSAGES IN BREAD ARE STILL IN THE TOP TEN LIST OF MY ELDEST DAUGHTER'S FAVE MEALS. CHECK OUT THE EXTRA SIZZLE IN THESE TRICKED UP HOTDOGS.

MAKES 6

1 small onion
1 tsp garlic paste
1 egg
1 cup (70g) stale breadcrumbs
2 tsp dried Italian herbs
500g sausages of your choice
1 tbsp extra virgin olive oil
2 cups (560g) bottled tomato passata
6 long white bread rolls
⅔ cup (70g) coarsely grated mozzarella
curly parsley leaves, to serve

Peel and grate onion. Place onion, garlic, egg, breadcrumbs and dried herbs in a large bowl. Squeeze sausage meat from casings into bowl. Season. Mix until well combined. Roll heaped tablespoons of mixture into balls to make 18 in total.

Heat half the oil in a large non-stick frying pan over medium heat. Add half the meatballs to pan. Cook, turning the meatballs with tongs, for 3 mins or until golden brown all over. Transfer meatballs to a plate. Repeat cooking with remaining oil and meatballs.

Return all meatballs to pan. Add passata and ¼ cup (60ml) water. Mix until combined; season. Simmer for 8 mins, stirring occasionally, or until the meatballs are cooked through.

Preheat grill to high.

Cut bread rolls in half lengthways, being careful not to cut all the way through. Spoon three meatballs and some sauce into each bread roll. Place the rolls on a large oven tray. Top meatballs with cheese.

Grill meatball subs for 2 mins or until cheese melts. Top with parsley and season with pepper.

Sauce
KETCH

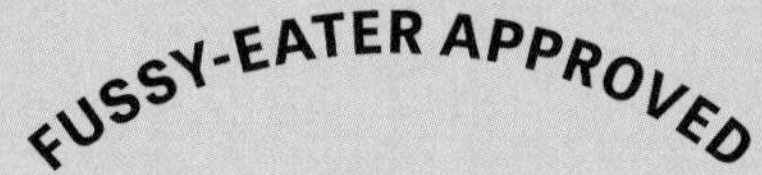

Pie maker party pies

PREP + COOK TIME 1 HOUR (+ COOLING)

SOMETHING ABOUT A PIE ALWAYS SAYS PARTY TIME TO ME. YOU CAN USE THE SAME TYPE OF PASTRY FOR THE TOP AND BOTTOM (I DO) HOWEVER THE COOKING WIZARDS TELL ME THAT USING TWO TYPES OF PASTRY PREVENTS SOGGY BOTTOMS AND GIVES YOU FLAKY TOPS.

MAKES 12

You will need a pie maker for this recipe.

1 tbsp olive oil
1 small onion, chopped finely
1 clove garlic, crushed
500g beef mince
400g can diced tomatoes
2 tbsp tomato paste
2 tbsp Worcestershire sauce
½ cup (125ml) beef stock
3 sheets frozen shortcrust pastry, thawed
3 sheets frozen puff pastry, thawed
1 egg, beaten lightly
2 tsp sesame seeds
tomato sauce, to serve

To make beef filling, heat oil in a large saucepan; cook onion, garlic and beef, stirring with a wooden spoon to break up any lumps, for 5 mins or until beef is well browned. Stir in tomatoes, paste, sauce and stock; bring to the boil. Reduce heat; simmer for 20 mins or until thickened. Season to taste. Cool. (Makes 3 cups.)

Lightly grease and preheat a 4-hole (⅓-cup/80ml) pie maker.

Using pastry cutter provided, cut 12 large rounds from shortcrust pastry and 12 small rounds from puff pastry. Line prepared holes with shortcrust pastry rounds, pressing pastry into base and side. Refrigerate remaining pastry rounds until required.

Spoon ¼ cup beef filling into each pastry case. Top with puff pastry rounds; press edges firmly to seal. Brush pastry with a little egg. Sprinkle with a third of the sesame seeds. Close lid; cook for 8 mins or until pastry is golden. Remove pies; transfer to a wire rack. Repeat, in batches, with remaining pastry rounds, beef filling, egg and sesame seeds to make 12 pies in total.

Serve pies with tomato sauce.

TIP Pies can be frozen for up to 3 months. Thaw in fridge overnight. Reheat pies in pie maker for 7 mins.

BARELY ANY PREP

No-burn, set & forget butter chicken

PREP TIME 15 MINUTES **COOK TIME** 3½ HOURS

ONCE I BROKE OUR SLOW COOKER BY TWISTING THE CONTROLS TOO MUCH BEFORE I HAD A CHANCE TO USE IT! THERE IS NOTHING HARD ABOUT MAKING THIS CHICKEN DISH, AND I LOVE HAVING DINNER READY WITH MINIMAL PREPARATION.

SERVES 4

You will need a slow cooker for this recipe.

8 skinless chicken thigh cutlets (1.6kg) (see tip)
2 x 450g jars butter chicken simmer sauce
400g can diced tomatoes
½ cup (140g) Greek yoghurt
2 Lebanese cucumbers, chopped finely
¼ cup mint leaves, shredded
steamed rice and garlic naan, to serve

Trim and discard excess fat from chicken.

Heat slow cooker on HIGH. Add chicken, simmer sauce and canned tomatoes. Cook, covered, for 3½ hours or until sauce reduces and chicken is very tender. Skim any fat from the surface with a spoon; discard. Season to taste.

Top butter chicken with yoghurt, cucumber and mint; season with pepper. Serve with steamed rice and garlic naan.

TIP If the chicken cutlets come with skin, remove the skin.

MID-WEEK WINNER

Rockstar salmon mornay

PREP + COOK TIME 45 MINUTES

A COMFORT MEAL THAT HAS ECHOES OF MY 80'S CHILDHOOD. SIMPLE TO MAKE AND SUPER TO TASTE. DON'T MISS MAKING A COMEBACK WITH THIS DISH!

SERVES 4

2 x 150g wood-roasted salmon portions
50g butter
1 onion, sliced thinly
1 tsp garlic paste
¼ cup (35g) plain flour
2 cups (500ml) milk, warmed
150g baby spinach leaves
2 tbsp coarsely chopped fresh dill, plus extra to serve
1 lemon, rind finely grated, then juiced
600g packaged mashed potato
⅓ cup (25g) finely grated parmesan

Preheat oven to 200°C/180°C fan-forced. Grease a shallow 2-litre (8-cup) ovenproof dish.

Peel away skin from salmon and discard, then flake salmon into large chunks.

Melt butter in a medium saucepan over medium-high heat; cook the onion and garlic, stirring, for 5 mins or until onion softens. Add flour; cook, stirring, for 1 min or until golden. Gradually stir in milk; cook, stirring, until mixture boils and thickens. Remove from heat; stir in spinach, flaked salmon, dill, lemon rind and juice. Season.

Spoon salmon mixture into dish; top with mash, sprinkle with parmesan, then season. Bake 25 mins or until top is golden. Sprinkle with extra dill to serve.

ROCKSTAR INGREDIENT Australian smoked salmon or ocean trout portions are the perfect 'I can't be bothered' ingredient.

MARGHERITA
FOUR CHEESES

SALAMI & OLIVES
PIZZA TABLE
RECIPE PAGES 116 & 117
PROSCIUTTO & ROCKET

Pizza table

PREP + COOK TIME 20 MINUTES

TONIGHT IS TAKEAWAY PIZZA, WELL SORT OF. USUALLY FRIDAY NIGHT WE PICK UP PIZZAS FROM OUR LOCAL ITALIAN RESTAURANT. IT'S A NIGHT OFF FROM COOKING FOR ME AND SIGNALS THE START OF THE WEEKEND.

HOWEVER THESE PIZZAS WILL MAKE A SPECIAL APPEARANCE THROUGH THE REST OF THE WEEK. MARGHERITA, AND SALAMI AND OLIVES FOR ME PLEASE!

EACH PIZZA SERVES 2

MARGHERITA

2 x classic pizza bases (300g)
½ cup (140g) tomato passata
150g bocconcini or mozzarella, sliced
¼ cup small basil leaves

Preheat oven to 220°C/200°C fan-forced. Place pizza bases on a large oven tray; spread with passata and top with cheese. Bake for 6-8 mins or until crust is golden brown and cheese is bubbling. Serve topped with basil leaves.

SALAMI & OLIVES

2 x classic pizza bases (300g)
½ cup (140g) Arrabbiata pasta sauce
150g thinly sliced salami
150g bocconcini or mozzarella, sliced
½ cup (60g) pitted Kalamata olives

Preheat oven to 220°C/200°C fan-forced. Place pizza bases on a large oven tray; spread with sauce and top with salami, cheese and olives. Bake for 6-8 mins or until crust is golden brown and cheese is bubbling.

FOUR CHEESES

2 x classic pizza bases (300g)
2 tbsp garlic-infused olive oil
1 cup (240g) fresh ricotta
125g each crumbled gorgonzola, grated parmesan and sliced bocconcini
1 tbsp chopped chives

Preheat oven to 220°C/200°C fan-forced. Place pizza bases on a large oven tray; brush with oil. Spread with ricotta, top with remaining cheeses. Bake for 6-8 mins or until crust is golden brown and cheese is bubbling. Serve topped with chives.

PROSCIUTTO & ROCKET

2 x classic pizza bases (300g)
½ cup (140g) passata
250g buffalo mozzarella, torn
100g mushrooms, sliced thinly
8 thin slices prosciutto (120g)
30g baby rocket leaves

Preheat oven to 220°C/200°C fan-forced. Place pizza bases on a large oven tray; spread with passata and top with mozzarella and sliced mushrooms. Bake for 6-8 mins or until crust is golden brown and cheese is bubbling. Serve topped with prosciutto and rocket.

Sweet Salvation

FUSSY-EATER APPROVED

Pancake cereal & berries

PREP + COOK TIME 30 MINUTES

STARTING MY DAY WITH SOMETHING SWEET IS PERFECT. ADD AS MANY TEENY PANCAKES AS YOU'D LIKE TO MINGLE WITH THE FRUIT. YOU COULD ALSO ENJOY THIS FOR DESSERT.

SERVES 4

2 eggs
1½ cups (375ml) buttermilk
¼ cup (55g) caster sugar
2 cups (300g) self-raising flour
½ tsp bicarbonate of soda
40g butter
berries or sliced banana, milk or yoghurt, and maple syrup, to serve

Process eggs, buttermilk, sugar and combined sifted flour and bicarb until smooth. Pour into a squeeze bottle, recycled condiment bottle or zip-top bag and seal it well. (If using a bag, tighten the loose part of the bag and secure with a peg or elastic band.)

Melt 1 tsp of the butter in a medium non-stick frying pan over medium heat. Squeeze (if using the bag method, first snip a small hole in one corner) mini 2cm rounds of pancake batter into the pan (don't worry if the sizes vary slightly). Cook pancakes for 1 min or until bubbles appear on the surface. Using two teaspoons flip pancakes over; cook other side until browned. Remove from pan. Repeat the process, using more butter between batches, until all the batter is used.

Divide pancake cereal and fruit among wide bowls. Serve with milk (or yoghurt) and maple syrup.

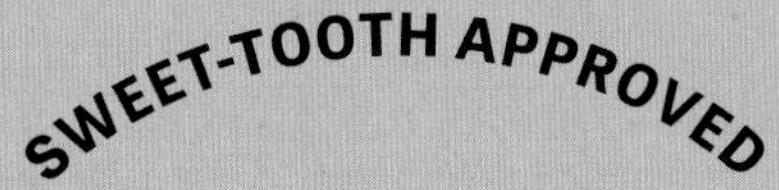

The disappearing frozen cheesecake tart

PREP TIME 25 MINUTES (+ FREEZING)

CHEESECAKE IS MY HUSBAND'S FAVOURITE DESSERT. (AND I LOVE ANYTHING AND EVERYTHING SWEET!) IT'S HARD TO STOP AT JUST ONE PIECE OF THIS SCRUMPTIOUS CHEESECAKE.

SERVES 8

90g butter
3 packets Red Velvet Oreo cookies (400g)
395g can sweetened condensed milk
750g cream cheese, at room temperature
1 tsp vanilla extract
canned whipped cream and sifted cocoa powder, to serve

Grease a 24cm (3-cup capacity) round metal pie dish.

Place butter in a microwave-safe bowl. Microwave on MEDIUM in 20-second bursts, stirring, until melted.

Place 1 packet Oreo cookies in a zip-lock plastic bag. Using a rolling pin, crush the cookies until coarse crumbs form. Set aside until needed.

Reserve 4 Oreos, then place remaining Oreos in the bowl of a food processor. Process until finely crushed. Add melted butter and process until well combined. Press into prepared pie dish to cover base and side, reaching to the top of the pie dish.

Place condensed milk, cream cheese and vanilla in cleaned food processor bowl. Process until smooth. Pour mixture into a large bowl. Stir through crushed Oreos until just combined. Pour cheesecake mixture into pie dish; smooth surface.

Freeze cheesecake for 5 hours or overnight until firm.

Stand at room temperature for 10 mins to soften slightly before serving. Halve the reserved Oreos.

Serve topped with whipped cream and halved Oreos; dust with cocoa powder.

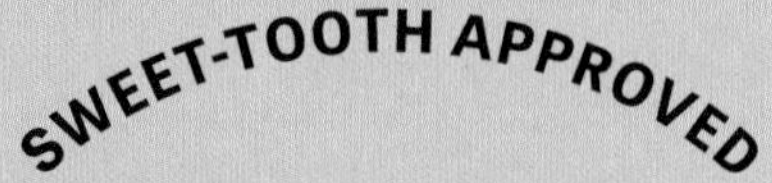

Caramel slice *is nice anytime*

PREP + COOK TIME 55 MINUTES (+ COOLING & REFRIGERATION)

OKAY I MIGHT HAVE SAID THAT I LOVE ALL THINGS SWEET, HOWEVER IF YOU TWISTED MY ARM I WOULD TELL YOU THAT CARAMEL SLICE IS THE WAY TO MY HEART. IF I HAD TO CHOOSE A LAST MEAL, IT WOULD BE CARAMEL SLICE.

MAKES 24

1 cup (150g) plain flour
½ cup (110g) firmly packed brown sugar
½ cup (40g) desiccated coconut
125g butter, melted
2 x 395g cans sweetened condensed milk
¼ cup (90g) golden syrup or treacle
125g butter, extra, chopped
200g milk or dark chocolate, chopped coarsely
2 tsp vegetable oil

Preheat oven to 180°C/160°C fan-forced. Grease a 20cm x 30cm rectangular slice pan; line base and long sides with baking paper, extending the paper 5cm over the sides.

Combine sifted flour, sugar and coconut in a bowl; stir in the melted butter. Press mixture firmly over base of pan. Bake for 15 mins or until light golden. Remove from oven; cool.

Place condensed milk, syrup and extra butter in a medium saucepan; stir over low heat until smooth. Pour mixture over cooled base. Bake for 20 mins or until golden brown. Cool.

Place chocolate and oil in a medium heatproof bowl over a medium saucepan of simmering water (make sure the base of the bowl doesn't touch the water); stir until smooth. Spread chocolate mixture over cooled slice. Refrigerate for 30 mins or until the chocolate is set before cutting with a hot knife.

TIP Store slice in an airtight container for up to 1 week. If the weather is hot, place the container in the fridge.

C

BARELY ANY PREP

Bickies *with power*

PREP + COOK TIME 30 MINUTES

A HIGHLIGHT OF MY CAREER WAS MEETING AND INTERVIEWING COOKIE MONSTER. HE HAS HIS PRIORITIES RIGHT WHEN IT COMES TO CHOCOLATE CHIP BICKIES. ONE IS NEVER ENOUGH.

MAKES 44

250g butter, softened
1 tsp vanilla extract
¾ cup (165g) caster sugar
¾ cup (165g) firmly packed brown sugar
1 egg
2¼ cups (335g) plain flour
1 tsp bicarbonate of soda
300g dark chocolate, chopped coarsely (see tips)
1 cup (20g) caramel popcorn, chopped coarsely

Preheat oven to 180°C/160°C fan-forced. Grease three oven trays; line with baking paper.

Beat butter, vanilla, sugars and egg in a medium bowl with an electric mixer until pale and fluffy. Transfer mixture to a large bowl; stir in sifted flour and bicarb, in two batches, until mixture is smooth. Stir in chocolate and popcorn.

Roll tablespoons of mixture into balls; place balls 5cm apart on trays.

Bake for 12 mins for a chewier biscuit or 14 mins until golden and crisp. Cool on trays.

TIPS You can also use Choc Melts or Choc Bits. Store these cookies in an airtight container for up to 1 week.

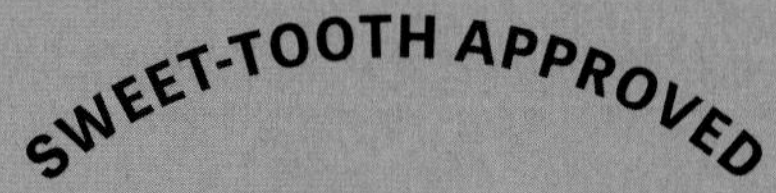

A pan & a whisk chocolate cake

PREP + COOK TIME 1 HOUR 25 MINUTES (+ COOLING)

YOU WON'T NEED ANY HEAVY-DUTY MIXERS FOR THIS SCRUMPTIOUS CAKE. BAKING CAN OFTEN BE HIT AND MISS WITH ME BUT THIS RECIPE NAILS IT.

SERVES 16

1 cup (220g) firmly packed brown sugar
½ cup (110g) caster sugar
250g butter, softened
3 eggs
1¼ cups (300g) sour cream
2 cups (300g) plain flour
⅓ cup (35g) cocoa powder
1 tsp bicarbonate of soda
180g dark chocolate, chopped coarsely
1 cup (160g) icing sugar
canned whipped cream
6 maraschino cherries with stalks

Preheat oven to 180°C/160°C fan-forced. Grease a 21cm round cake pan; line base and side with baking paper, extending the paper 5cm over the sides.

Place sugars, half the butter and ½ cup (125ml) boiling water in a saucepan; stir over medium heat until sugar dissolves. Remove from heat; cool slightly, then whisk in eggs and ⅔ cup (160g) sour cream until combined. Sift over dry ingredients, then whisk briefly until no lumps of flour are visible. Pour mixture into cake pan and spread smoothly.

Bake cake for 50 mins or until a skewer inserted into the centre comes out clean. Leave cake in pan for 10 mins before turning, top-side up, onto a wire rack to cool.

Meanwhile, to make the chocolate glaze, whisk chocolate, icing sugar and remaining butter and sour cream in a medium saucepan over low heat for 2 mins or until melted and smooth. Transfer the mixture to a small bowl; cool 15 mins. Refrigerate for 30 mins or until glaze is spreadable.

Spread cold cake with chocolate glaze. Top with swirls of whipped cream and maraschino cherries. Serve with extra cherries, if you like.

Happy Birthday

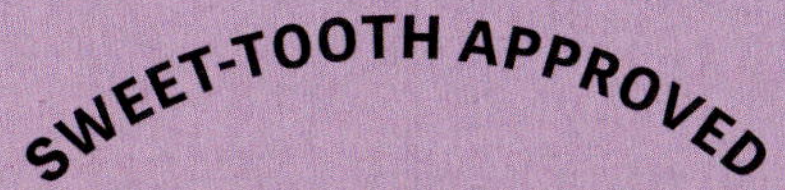

Happy birthday to me!

PREP + COOK TIME 1 HOUR (+ FREEZING & COOLING)

WHAT SORT OF CAKE DOES A CRAZY CAT LADY LOVE? GUESS? THE JOY HERE IS IN THE DECORATING – NO BAKING REQUIRED. (AND THE MUSK STICK ICING ON THIS CAKE!)

SERVES 12-14

3 x 600g store-bought round white mud cakes
28 musk sticks
⅓ cup (80ml) milk, approximately
250g unsalted butter, softened
3 cups (480g) icing sugar, sifted
pink food colouring
1 purple jelly bean, halved lengthways
1 white marshmallow, halved horizontally
10cm piece black licorice strap
67 Smarties
4 purple jubes, halved horizontally
2 tbsp 100's & 1000's

Freeze cakes for 2 hours to firm.

To make icing, break 25 musk sticks into small pieces. Place in a microwave-safe bowl with ¼ cup (60ml) milk. Microwave on HIGH in 30-second bursts, stirring, until smooth. Cool. Beat butter in a bowl with an electric mixer until as white as possible. Gradually beat in sugar, musk stick mixture and remaining milk in two batches. Tint pink with colouring, mix well.

Level cake tops, removing icing; discard. Using image as a guide, cut a 4cm half-moon-shaped piece from one side of a cake for tail, then a 5cm piece from bottom; cut in half for ears. For head, cut a 14cm round from a second cake using a plate as a guide. Place third cake, cut-side down, on a cake board for body; add head, ears and tail, cut-side down, to resemble a cat, securing with icing. Spread top and sides of cat with most of the remaining icing.

Glue jelly bean halves to marshmallow halves with icing for eyes; add to cake. Using scissors, cut a 2cm triangle for nose and two 4cm strips for mouth from licorice; add to cake. Using picture as a guide, place Smarties for belly, jubes for collar and 100's & 1000's for inner ears. Halve the remaining musk sticks lengthways for whiskers; add to cake.

TIP If the icing becomes firm on standing, add a little extra milk to achieve the desired consistency.

Sunbeam

HIDDEN VEGIES

Food-processor carrot cake

PREP + COOK TIME 1¾ HOURS (+ COOLING)

CARROT CAKE IS MY YOUNGEST DAUGHTER'S PICK OF THE SWEET TREATS. NOTHING BEATS THE CREAM CHEESE FROSTING AND CARROT COMBO.

SERVES 12

3 large carrots (540g)
1 cup (120g) pecans, plus extra to serve
3 eggs
1⅓ cups (295g) firmly packed brown sugar
1 cup (250ml) vegetable oil
2½ cups (375g) self-raising flour
½ tsp bicarbonate of soda
2 tsp mixed spice, plus extra to serve
3⅓ cups (540g) icing sugar
125g butter, softened
250g cream cheese, softened
2 tsp finely grated lemon rind

Preheat oven to 180°C/160°C fan-forced. Grease two 22cm round cake pans; line bases and sides with baking paper.

Using the grater attachment of a food processor, grate carrots. Measure 3 packed cups and place in a large bowl. (Alternatively grate with a box grater.) Wash and dry the food processor.

Place pecans in the food processor; pulse until coarsely chopped. Add to bowl with carrots.

Place eggs, sugar and oil in food processor bowl; process for 3 mins or until thick and creamy. Pour over the carrot mixture and stir to combine. Sift over flour, bicarb and mixed spice; stir to combine. Pour mixture equally between pans.

Bake cakes for 45 mins or until a skewer inserted into the centre comes out clean. Leave cakes in pans for 5 mins before transferring to a wire rack to cool.

Meanwhile, to make cream cheese frosting, in clean food processor bowl, process the icing sugar until smooth. Add butter, cream cheese and lemon rind; process for 5 mins, scraping down the side of the bowl occasionally, until smooth.

Place one cake on a plate, spread with half the frosting. Top with remaining cake; spread top with remaining frosting. Decorate with extra pecans. Dust with a little extra mixed spice.

Spar-letta

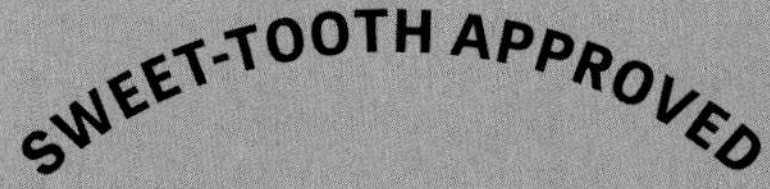

Rock my road

PREP TIME 20 MINUTES (+ REFRIGERATION)

ME-TIME IS READING IN BED WHILE MUNCHING ON CHOCOLATE. ALTHOUGH SHARING IS CARING I DON'T WANT TO SHARE THIS ROCKY ROAD WITH ANYONE.

MAKES 16

600g milk or dark chocolate, chopped finely
1½ tbsp vegetable oil
100g mini marshmallows
140g raspberry lollies
130g caramel nut popcorn
⅔ cup (50g) shredded coconut, toasted
½ cup (70g) slivered almonds, roasted
100g chocolate-coated honeycomb, chopped coarsely

Grease a 20cm square cake pan; line base and sides with baking paper, extending the paper 5cm over the sides.

Place 200g of the chocolate in a microwave-safe bowl. Microwave on HIGH in 30-second bursts, stirring, until melted and smooth. Pour into base of pan. Leave to partially set.

Place remaining chocolate and the oil in a microwave-safe bowl. Microwave on HIGH in 30-second bursts, stirring, until just melted and smooth.

Combine remaining ingredients in a large heatproof bowl, reserving 1 cup of the mixture to scatter over the top at the end. Add the melted chocolate to remaining mixture; stir until well combined.

Spread chocolate mixture into pan. Scatter with reserved mixture, pressing lightly into chocolate.

Refrigerate for 2 hours or until set. Lift rocky road from pan and cut into 16 pieces with a hot knife.

TIP Rocky road will keep for up to 1 week in an airtight container in the fridge.

BARELY ANY PREP

No-bake Mars bar slice

PREP + COOK TIME 30 MINUTES (+ REFRIGERATION)

HOW CAN YOU IMPROVE A MARS BAR? THE ANSWER IS CHOCOLATE, ALWAYS MORE CHOCOLATE! AND THE RICE BUBBLES ADD SOME EXTRA CRUNCH.

MAKES 14

5 x 47g Mars bars, chopped
100g unsalted butter, chopped
3 cups (105g) Rice Bubbles
200g dark or milk chocolate, chopped
2 tsp vegetable oil
chopped honeycomb, to decorate (optional)

Grease a 20cm x 30cm slice pan. Line base and long sides with baking paper, extending the paper 5cm above edge of pan.

Place the chopped Mars bar and butter in a medium saucepan. Stir over low heat for 5 mins or until melted. Place the Rice Bubbles in a large heatproof bowl. Add Mars bar mixture; stir to combine. Press mixture firmly into pan. Refrigerate for 2 hours or until firm.

Combine the chocolate and oil in a heatproof bowl. Place bowl over a medium saucepan of simmering water (make sure base of bowl doesn't touch water); stir until chocolate is melted and smooth. Spread chocolate mixture evenly over slice. Sprinkle with honeycomb, if using. Refrigerate 1 hour or until set.

Using a hot knife, cut into small bars.

TIPS The mixture may look separated when melting the Mars bars and butter, but will come back together after stirring for about 5 mins. Store slice in an airtight container in the fridge.

C

Movie night banana splits with sprinkles

PREP TIME 20 MINUTES (+ FREEZING & REFRIGERATION)

OLD-SCHOOL BANANA SPLITS TAKE ME BACK TO MY DAYDREAMS OF WANTING TO BE SANDY IN THE MOVIE GREASE!

SERVES 4

4 medium bananas
200g milk chocolate, chopped
1 tbsp coconut oil
¼ cup (55g) 100's & 1000's
4 scoops (240ml) chocolate ice-cream
4 scoops (240ml) vanilla ice-cream
4 scoops (240ml) strawberry ice-cream
250g can whipped cream
4 maraschino cherries with stalks

Line a large tray with baking paper. Peel bananas and cut in half crossways. Lay bananas on tray in a single layer; freeze for 1 hour.

Place chocolate and coconut oil in a small microwave-safe jug; microwave on MEDIUM in 30-second bursts, stirring, until the chocolate is melted. Cool slightly. Dip each banana half three-quarters of the way up in chocolate then return to lined tray. Sprinkle with 100's & 1000's. Refrigerate 15 mins to set chocolate.

Place two chocolate coated banana halves in each of four dishes; place a scoop of chocolate, vanilla and strawberry ice-cream between banana halves in each dish.

Pipe cream on top of ice-cream scoops; top with cherries, sprinkle with any remaining 100's & 1000's.

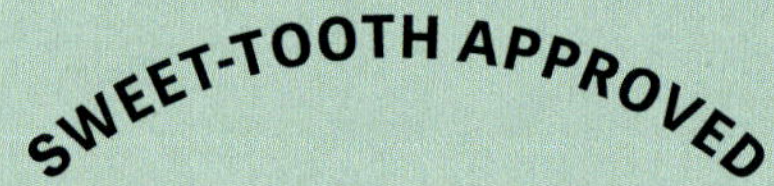

Lamington cake

PREP + COOK TIME 45 MINUTES (+ COOLING)

WHAT'S BETTER THAN A LAMINGTON? A GIANT LAMINGTON, OF COURSE. WHY? BECAUSE IT'S MUCH EASIER TO MAKE THIS CAKE VERSION!

SERVES 8

6 eggs
1 cup (220g) caster sugar
1 cup (150g) self-raising flour
½ cup (75g) cornflour
¼ tsp salt
20g butter, at room temperature
2 cups (320g) icing sugar mixture
½ cup (50g) cocoa powder
½ cup (125ml) milk
½ cup (160g) raspberry jam
300ml thickened cream, whipped
1½ cups (115g) shredded coconut

Preheat oven to 180°C/160°C fan-forced. Grease 2 x 20cm square cake pans; line bases with baking paper.

Beat eggs in a large bowl using an electric mixer until fluffy. Add the caster sugar; beat for 8-10 mins or until thick and pale.

Sift combined flours and salt twice onto a sheet of baking paper, then scatter over egg mixture. Using a large metal spoon, gently fold through egg mixture.

Combine half the butter and ⅓ cup (80ml) boiling water in a small heatproof bowl. Add to cake mixture; quickly fold through. Pour mixture evenly into pans. Bake 18 mins or until golden and a skewer inserted into the centre comes out clean. Turn cakes out onto a wire rack to cool.

To make the icing, sift icing sugar mixture and cocoa into large bowl. Add milk, remaining butter and 2 tbsp boiling water; whisk until smooth.

Sandwich cooled cakes together with jam and cream. Place on a wire rack over an oven tray. Pour icing over cake to cover top and sides completely, allowing excess to drip off onto tray. Sprinkle generously with coconut, pressing onto sides as well.

TIP If preferred, use a store-bought unfilled sponge cake instead of making your own.

BARELY ANY PREP

Tutti frutti trifle

PREP TIME 25 MINUTES (+ REFRIGERATION)

THIS TRIFLE IS RETRO AND REMARKABLY EASY TO MAKE. ANYTHING WITH JELLY IS FOR ME, AND JAM ROLLS TAKE ME BACK TO AFTERNOON TEA TREATS AS A LITTLE GIRL.

SERVES 8-10

3 x 85g packets raspberry jelly crystals
1 tray ice-cubes
250g packet mini jam sponge rolls
410g can peach slices in juice
432g can pineapple slices in juice
800g bottle Farmhouse vanilla custard
2 x 250g tubs mascarpone
6 maraschino cherries with stems
shaved chocolate, to serve

Place jelly crystals in a 2-litre (8-cup) heatproof jug. Add 2 cups (500ml) boiling water; whisk until crystals dissolve. Add ice-cubes; whisk until ice cubes melt. Add enough cold water (approx. 3 cups/750ml) so liquid level reaches the 1.25 litre mark on the jug. The jelly should be the consistency of thick egg white. (If it's not, simply refrigerate until thickened.)

Cut each mini jam sponge roll into five slices.

To assemble trifle, press a ring of jam roll slices flat to the inside of a glass 3.5-litre (14-cup) serving dish. Fill centre with remaining slices to support them. Carefully pour in thickened jelly, without disturbing the placement of jam roll slices. Cover and refrigerate for 4 hours or until set.

To serve, drain the peach and pineapple slices. Pat dry with paper towel, then halve pineapple slices. Arrange alternate pieces of fruit around the edge of the serving dish over set jelly, then fill the centre with remaining fruit.

Place custard and mascarpone in a large bowl of an electric mixer; whisk on medium speed until almost firm peaks form. Spoon custard mixture over fruit in pillowy mounds. Top with maraschino cherries and shaved chocolate.

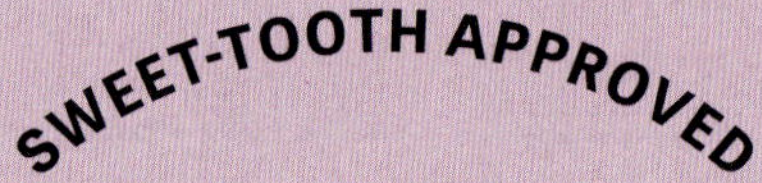

Unicorn coconut ice

PREP TIME 20 MINUTES (+ REFRIGERATION)

SUGAR AND UNICORNS! IS THERE A MORE PERFECT MATCH? I DON'T THINK SO – ESPECIALLY WHEN COCONUT ICE IS INVOLVED.

MAKES 64

5¼ cups (840g) icing sugar
2½ cups (200g) desiccated coconut
395g can sweetened condensed milk
1 egg white, beaten lightly
pink food colouring
¼ cup (55g) unicorn sprinkles

Grease a 19cm square cake pan; line base and sides with baking paper, extending the paper 5cm over the sides.

Sift icing sugar into a large bowl; stir in coconut, then condensed milk and egg white until almost combined. Using your hands, finish combining the ingredients well.

Divide mixture into two bowls; tint one mixture with pink colouring. Press white mixture into pan; level the surface. Top with pink mixture; level the surface. Scatter with sprinkles, pressing them down slightly into the mix.

Cover pan; refrigerate for 3 hours or until set before cutting into squares.

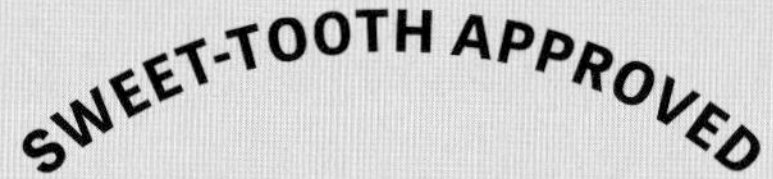

Carmen Miranda pavlova

PREP + COOK TIME 2½ HOURS (+ COOLING)

PAVLOVA IS SOMETHING I HAVE MASTERED! MY SECRET – KEEP THE ELECTRIC MIXER ON A LOW SPEED WHEN BEATING THE EGG WHITES. YOU'LL GET A GLOSSY MERINGUE EACH TIME.

SERVES 10

6 egg whites
pinch cream of tartar
1½ cups (330g) caster sugar
3 tsp cornflour
2 tsp vanilla bean paste
1½ tsp white vinegar
1¾ cups (430ml) thickened cream
500g fruit of your choice (berries, pomegranate seeds, peaches, nectarines, passionfruit)
icing sugar, to serve

Preheat oven to 120°C/100°C fan-forced. Grease an oven tray. Mark a 20cm circle on a sheet of baking paper; place paper, marked-side down, on tray.

Whisk egg whites and cream of tartar in a bowl with an electric mixer until soft peaks form. Gradually add caster sugar, beating until sugar has dissolved after each addition and mixture is thick and glossy. (I've found that beating on a low speed only in a glass or ceramic bowl, never plastic, avoids the meringue cracking later.) Fold in sifted cornflour, then vanilla and vinegar. Spread meringue inside marked round on tray; build up the side to about 10cm high and flatten the top.

Bake pavlova for 1¾ hours or until dry to touch. Turn oven off; cool pavlova in oven with door ajar.

Just before serving, beat cream in a small bowl with electric mixer until soft peaks form. Spoon cream on pavlova, top with fruit. Dust with icing sugar.

TIP Pavlova can be baked a day ahead; store in an airtight container in a cool dry place. Assemble with cream and fruit close to serving.

CAN'T BE BOTHERED

Cobbled together cobbler

PREP + COOK TIME 40 MINUTES

HOW TO MAKE A CAKE WHEN YOU'RE NOT REALLY BAKING AT ALL. IT'S THE PERFECT ZERO-WASHING-UP, NON-COOKING PERSON'S RECIPE.

SERVES 6

835g canned fruit, drained (peaches, apricots, pineapple, apples or pears)
440g packet golden buttercake mix (see tips)
125g chilled butter, sliced thinly
1 tsp ground cinnamon
topping of your choice, to serve (ice-cream, custard, cream or yoghurt)

Preheat oven to 180°C/160°C fan-forced.

Arrange your chosen fruit over the base of a large, ovenproof frying pan. Sprinkle evenly with the dry buttercake mix and top evenly with the sliced butter; sprinkle with cinnamon.

Bake for 30 mins or until the cake mixture is browned and the centre is firm.

Serve cobbler with topping of your choice.

TIPS Packet cake mix is the rockstar ingredient of this recipe. This time ignore the ingredients called for on the packet. If you like, the icing sugar sachet can be used to dust the finished cobbler.

BARELY ANY PREP

Possible impossible coconut & passionfruit pie

PREP + COOK TIME 1 HOUR

IMPRESS EVERYONE WITH THIS GENIUS PIE RECIPE. IT'S ONLY 'IMPOSSIBLE' BECAUSE OF THE WAY THE INGREDIENTS MAGICALLY SEPARATE INTO THREE LAYERS DURING BAKING. THE HEAVIER FLOUR SINKS TO THE BASE A BIT LIKE PASTRY, WHILE THE LIGHTER COCONUT FLOATS FORMING A TOP AND THE EGG AND MILK FORM A CUSTARD LAYER IN THE MIDDLE.

SERVES 8

½ cup (75g) plain flour
1 cup (220g) caster sugar
¾ cup (60g) desiccated coconut
4 eggs
1 tsp vanilla extract
125g butter, melted
2 passionfruit, pulp removed
½ cup (40g) flaked almonds
2 cups (500ml) milk
icing sugar and pouring cream, to serve

Preheat oven to 180°C/160°C fan-forced. Grease a deep 24cm (3-cup capacity) pie dish.

Combine sifted flour, caster sugar, coconut, eggs, vanilla, butter, passionfruit and half the almonds in a large bowl. Gradually add milk, stirring until combined. Pour mixture into pie dish.

Bake pie for 35 mins. Remove from oven, sprinkle with remaining almonds; bake for a further 15 mins or until browned lightly and set.

Dust pie with icing sugar and serve with cream.

WAFFLES À LA SUZETTE
RECIPE PAGES 156 & 157

BARELY ANY PREP

Waffles à la Suzette

PREP + COOK TIME 20 MINUTES

THIS SWEET TRIUMPH IS INSPIRED BY CRÊPES SUZETTE (MINUS THE ALCOHOL). DETAILS AROUND WHO SUZETTE WAS AND WHY SHE HAD A SAUCE NAMED AFTER HER ARE PRETTY SKETCHY, WITH THEORIES RANGING FROM SHE WAS ROYALTY TO AN ACTRESS. REGARDLESS, MY FAMILY LOVE IT WHEN I GIVE THIS EXTRAVAGANZA A WHIRL.

TO TRANSFORM THIS RECIPE FROM PLATED DESSERT TO WAFFLE SMORGASBORD, PICK FROM THE EXTRAS LIST AND PRESENT ALL THE ELEMENTS SEPARATELY ON THE TABLE. THAT WAY EVERYONE CAN MAKE THEIR OWN FLAVOUR COMBOS AND CREATE THEIR OWN MOMENTS OF JOY.

FOR THE ULTIMATE INDULGENCE, SERVE 2 WAFFLES PER PERSON. OR IF YOU'VE GOT MORE MOUTHS TO FEED GO WITH 1 WAFFLE EACH – YOU CAN ALWAYS GO OVER-THE-TOP WITH THE TOPPINGS!

SERVES 4

125g butter
½ cup (110g) caster sugar
2 tsp finely grated orange rind
½ cup (125ml) orange juice
2 medium oranges, peeled, sliced thinly into rounds
8 Belgian-style plain or chocolate chip waffles (480g)
250g can whipped cream or ice-cream of your choice
2 tbsp toasted flaked almonds
extras sauces: Nutella (warmed and thinned to a sauce with boiling water), caramel sauce
extras toppings: M&M's, smashed chocolate bars, berries, nuts, 100's & 1000's

To make the Suzette sauce, melt butter in a small heavy-based saucepan. Add sugar, orange rind and juice; cook, stirring, over low heat, without boiling, until sugar dissolves. Bring to the boil. Reduce heat; simmer, without stirring, for 2 mins or until sauce thickens slightly. Add orange slices; cook for 2 mins or until orange has softened slightly.

Warm waffles according to packet directions.

Divide waffles among serving plates; top with whipped cream, orange slices, Suzette sauce, almonds and any other sauces or toppings of your choice.

TIP For an adult version, stir 2 tbsp orange-flavoured liqueur into Suzette sauce with the orange juice.

Glossary

BREADCRUMBS, PANKO also known as Japanese breadcrumbs. Available in two types: larger pieces and fine crumbs; both have a lighter texture than Western-style breadcrumbs.

BUTTERMILK made from no-fat or low-fat milk to which specific bacterial cultures have been added.

CHEESE

cream a soft cow-milk cheese, its fat content ranges from 14 to 33%.

mascarpone an Italian fresh cultured cream product. Has a soft, creamy buttery-rich, luscious texture.

mozzarella soft, spun-curd cheese. The most popular pizza cheese because of its low melting point and elasticity when heated.

parmesan a hard, grainy cow-milk cheese. Reggiano is the best variety.

ricotta a soft, sweet, moist, white cow-milk cheese with a low fat content and a slightly grainy texture. The name roughly translates as 'cooked again' and refers to ricotta's manufacture from a whey that is itself a by-product of other cheese making.

CHIVES related to the onion and leek; has a subtle onion flavour. Used more for flavour than as an ingredient.

CHOCOLATE, DARK made of a high percentage of cocoa liquor and cocoa butter, and little added sugar.

CINNAMON available in pieces (sticks or quills) and ground into powder; used as a sweet, fragrant flavouring for both sweet and savoury foods.

COCOA, POWDER cocoa beans (cacao seeds) that have been fermented, roasted, shelled, ground into powder then cleared of most of the fat content.

COCONUT

desiccated concentrated, dried, unsweetened and shredded coconut flesh.

shredded unsweetened thin strips of dried coconut flesh.

CORIANDER bright-green-leafed herb with a pungent flavour. Also available ground or as seeds; these should not be substituted for fresh coriander as the tastes are different.

CORNFLOUR available made from corn or wheat (wheaten cornflour gives a lighter texture in cakes); used as a thickening agent in cooking.

CREAM

pouring contains no additives. Has a minimum fat content of 35%.

sour thick, commercially cultured sour cream with a minimum fat content of 35%.

thickened a whipping cream that contains a thickener. It has a minimum fat content of 35%.

CUMIN the dried seed of a plant related to the parsley family. Available dried as seeds or ground. It has a spicy, almost curry-like flavour.

DILL used fresh or dried, in seed form or ground. Its anise/celery sweetness flavours the food of the Scandinavian countries, and Germany and Greece. Its feathery, frond-like fresh leaves are grassier and more subtle than the dried version or the seeds.

FENNEL a white to very pale green-white, firm, crisp, roundish vegetable about 8-12cm in diameter. The bulb has a slightly sweet, anise flavour but the leaves have a much stronger taste.

GOCHUJANG a Korean fermented red chilli paste, available in major supermarkets.

GOLDEN SYRUP a by-product of refined sugarcane; maple syrup or honey can be substituted.

LEMONGRASS a tall, clumping, lemon-smelling and tasting, sharp-edged aromatic tropical grass. Can be found fresh, dried, powdered and frozen, in supermarkets, greengrocers and Asian food shops.

MUSTARD

Dijon pale brown, creamy, distinctively flavoured, fairly mild French mustard.

wholegrain a coarse-grain mustard which is made from crushed mustard seeds and Dijon-style French mustard.

OIL

olive made from ripened olives. Extra virgin and virgin are the first and second press, respectively; 'extra light' or 'light' refers to taste not fat levels.

vegetable oils sourced from plant fats.

ONIONS

green also known, incorrectly, as shallots; an immature onion picked before the bulb has formed, having a long, bright-green edible stalk.

eschalots also called shallots; small and brown-skinned.

OREGANO a herb having a woody stalk and clumps of tiny, dark-green leaves. Has a peppery flavour.

OYSTER SAUCE Asian in origin, this thick, richly flavoured brown sauce is made from oysters and their brine, cooked with salt and soy sauce, and thickened with starches.

PAPRIKA ground dried sweet red capsicum; there are many grades and types available, including sweet, hot, mild and smoked.

PARSLEY an extremely versatile herb with a fresh, slightly earthy flavour. The flat-leaf variety (also known as continental or Italian parsley) is stronger in flavour and darker in colour than curly parsley.

PASSATA sieved tomato puree. To substitute, puree and sieve canned tomatoes or use canned tomato puree which is similar, but slightly thicker.

SOY SAUCE made from fermented soybeans. Several variations are available in supermarkets and Asian food stores.

SUGAR, PALM made from the sap of the sugar palm tree. Light brown to black in colour and usually sold in rock-hard cakes; use brown sugar if unavailable.

TURMERIC related to galangal and ginger; known for the golden colour it imparts. When fresh turmeric is called for in a recipe, you can use the more commonly found dried powder instead.

VANILLA

extract obtained from vanilla beans infused in water; a non-alcoholic version of essence.

paste made from vanilla pods; contains real seeds. Highly concentrated; 1 tsp replaces a whole vanilla pod.

VINEGAR, BALSAMIC there are many balsamic vinegars on the market ranging in pungency and quality, depending on how long they have been aged. Deep rich brown in colour. Has a sweet/sour flavour.

WORCESTERSHIRE SAUCE thin, dark brown spicy sauce developed by the British when in India; used as a seasoning and a condiment.

YOGHURT, GREEK plain yoghurt that has been strained in a cloth to remove the whey and to give it a creamy consistency.

ZUCCHINI also known as courgette; belongs to the squash family.

Sugar

Conversion Chart

MEASURES

One Australian metric measuring cup holds approximately 250ml; one Australian metric tablespoon holds 20ml; one Australian metric teaspoon holds 5ml.

The difference between one country's measuring cups and another's is within a two- or three-teaspoon variance and will not affect your cooking results. North America, New Zealand and the United Kingdom use a 15ml tablespoon. All cup and spoon measurements are level.

The most accurate way of measuring dry ingredients is to weigh them.

When measuring liquids, use a clear glass or plastic jug with the metric markings.

We use extra-large eggs with an average weight of 60g.

OVEN TEMPERATURES

The oven temperatures in this book are for conventional and fan-forced ovens.

	°C (Celsius)	°F (Fahrenheit)
Very slow	120	250
Slow	150	300
Moderately slow	160	325
Moderate	180	350
Moderately hot	200	400
Hot	220	425
Very hot	240	475

DRY MEASURES

metric	imperial
15g	½oz
30g	1oz
60g	2oz
90g	3oz
125g	4oz (¼lb)
155g	5oz
185g	6oz
220g	7oz
250g	8oz (½lb)
280g	9oz
315g	10oz
345g	11oz
375g	12oz (¾lb)
410g	13oz
440g	14oz
470g	15oz
500g	16oz (1lb)
750g	24oz (1½lb)
1kg	32oz (2lb)

LIQUID MEASURES

metric	imperial
30ml	1 fluid oz
60ml	2 fluid oz
100ml	3 fluid oz
125ml	4 fluid oz
150ml	5 fluid oz
190ml	6 fluid oz
250ml	8 fluid oz
300ml	10 fluid oz
500ml	16 fluid oz
600ml	20 fluid oz
1000ml (1 litre)	1¾ pints

LENGTH MEASURES

metric	imperial
3mm	⅛in
6mm	¼in
1cm	½in
2cm	¾in
2.5cm	1in
5cm	2in
6cm	2½in
8cm	3in
10cm	4in
13cm	5in
15cm	6in
18cm	7in
20cm	8in
22cm	9in
25cm	10in
28cm	11in
30cm	12in (1ft)

Index

Published in 2023 by Are Media Books, Australia.
Are Media Books is a division of Are Media Pty Ltd.

ARE MEDIA
Chief executive officer Jane Huxley

ARE MEDIA BOOKS
Group publisher Nicole Byers
Editorial & food director Sophia Young
Books director David Scotto
Creative director & designer Hannah Blackmore
Managing editor Stephanie Kistner
Junior editor Georgia Moore
Food editor Sophia Young

Food photography
Photographer John Paul Urizar
Stylist Kate Brown
Photochefs Clare Maguire, Rebecca Lyall
Lifestyle photography
Photographer Peter Brew-Bevan
Stylist Jerrie-Joy Redman-Lloyd
Photochef Clare Maguire
Hair and makeup Normie Gonzales
Wardrobe stylist Mattie Cronan

Printed in China by
Leo Paper Products.

A catalogue record for this book is available from the National Library of Australia.
ISBN 978-1-76122-067-8

Published by Are Media Books, a division of Are Media Pty Limited, 54 Park St, Sydney; GPO Box 4088, Sydney, NSW 2001, Australia
Ph +61 2 9282 8000;
www.awwcookbooks.com.au

International rights enquiries
internationalrights@aremedia.com.au

Order books
phone 1300 322 007 (within Australia) or order online at
www.awwcookbooks.com.au

Send recipe enquiries to
recipeenquiries@aremedia.com.au

TRUSTED BRANDS USED IN OUR TEST KITCHEN

womensweeklyfood

@womensweeklyfood

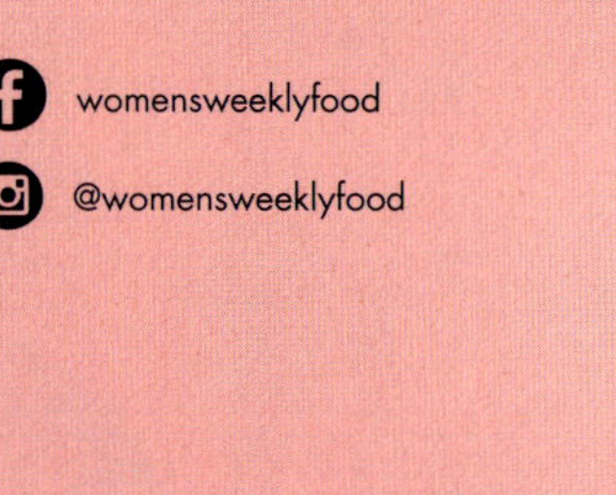